# EARTH, INC.

R. BUCKMINSTER FULLER is the world-famous inventor of the geodesic dome. His distinguished career has taken him all over Spaceship Earth, where he has been consultant to governmental and private agencies, and adviser to a wide range of intellectual and political leaders. He has been Distinguished University Professor at Southern Illinois University since 1959. He is a Fellow of the Royal Society of Arts; Fellow, American Association for the Advancement of Science; and former Charles Eliot Norton Professor of Poetry at Harvard University. Among his recent honors are Britain's 1967 Royal Gold Medal for Architecture, the 1968 Gold Medal Award of the National Institute of Arts and Letters, and the American Institute of Architects' 1970 Gold Medal.

Mr. Fuller is the author of *No More Secondhand God, Nine Chains to the Moon, Utopia or Oblivion, Ideas and Integrities, Untitled Epic Poem on the History of Industrialization, Operating Manual for Spaceship Earth,* and most recently, *Intuition.*

# R. Buckminster Fuller
# EARTH, INC.

Anchor Books
ANCHOR PRESS/DOUBLEDAY
Garden City, New York

The Anchor Books edition is the first edition of EARTH, INC.

Anchor Books edition: 1973

EARTH, INC., originally published by the Fuller Research Foundation, New York, 1947.

THE LEONARDO TYPE, originally published by the Jawaharlal Nehru Memorial Fund, 1969, as part II of *Planetary Planning*.

EARTHIANS' CRITICAL MOMENT, TELEGRAM TO SENATOR EDMUND MUSKIE, and TEN PROPOSALS FOR IMPROVING THE WORLD all appeared in the New York *Times*.

REVOLUTION IN WOMBLAND and INEXORABLE EVOLUTION AND HUMAN ECOLOGY appeared as the introduction to Gene Youngblood's *Expanded Cinema*, E. P. Dutton & Co., Inc., New York, 1970.

VERTICAL IS TO LIVE—HORIZONTAL IS TO DIE originally appeared in *The American Scholar*, Vol. 39, No. 1, Winter, 1969–70.

GO IN TO GO OUT, originally published in *World*, July 18, 1972.

# CONTENTS

# What I am trying to do

Acutely aware of our beings' limitations and acknowledging the infinite mystery of the a priori Universe into which we are born but nevertheless searching for a conscious means of hopefully competent participation by humanity in its own evolutionary trending while employing only the unique advantages inhering exclusively to those individuals who take and maintain the economic initiative in the face of the formidable physical capital and credit advantages of the massive corporations and political states and deliberately avoiding political ties and tactics while endeavoring by experiments and explorations to excite individuals' awareness and realization of humanity's higher potentials I seek through comprehensive anticipatory design science and its reductions to physical practices to reform the environment instead of trying to reform humans, being intent thereby to accomplish prototyped capabilities of doing more with less whereby in turn the wealth augmenting prospects of such design science regenerations will induce their spontaneous and economically successful industrial proliferation by world around services' managements all of which chain reaction provoking events will both permit and induce all humanity to realize full lasting economic and physical success plus enjoyment of all the Earth without one individual interfering with or being advantaged at the expense of another.                                    **R. Buckminster Fuller**

# EARTH, INC.

# EARTH, INC.*

## Synopsis and Preface

This chart portrays the net physical wealth accomplishments of man's civilized history.

Speaking figuratively, this chart is man's cosmic report card for his enrollment as a freshman in the One World University. In this figurative sense, it may be verified easily at the Pearly Gates, for the checklist includes only universal and infinite principles for grading reference. This report abandons reference to man's successes within the framework of his self-invented systems—of required performance in Earth Incorporated. In Earth, Inc., the laws, superstitions and values may be altered and relabeled by man himself and may not be at all acceptable to St. Peter, who can scarcely keep up with the daily shifts of expediency in the playing rules. This cosmic report card records man's degree of discovery and mastery of the unlabeled universal phenomena which are everywhere potential to his command if he is wise enough to apprehend their finite existence and comprehend their infinite significance. The physical significance is that these unlabeled potentials pay

* Originally published by the Fuller Research Foundation, New York, 1947. This item should be read in conjunction with the chart entitled "Profile of the Industrial Revolution." Original chart of 1943 corrected to 1970 in 1972.

off, by increasing the universal and absolute degree of humanity's advantage over circumstance and fate, rather than by rearranging the local and relative survival circumstances of individuals. Thus St. Peter may (as, for that matter, so may we) mark man's performance paper against a specific schedule of irrefutable and measurable opportunities.

The report card covers a period of 700 years, from A.D. 1250 to 1970. It commences at 1250 because in that year man consciously isolated a chemical element. This was the first time in those annals of total history now available to man that he had made such a discovery and accomplished elemental separation from contiguous elements. He did not phrase it that way at the time, but that is what he actually accomplished.

Man had already, at some prehistoric time, accomplished the selective use (if not the isolation) of nine out of the full family of ninety-two chemical elements, viz., iron, lead, carbon, tin, silver, mercury, gold, sulphur and copper. The newly isolated element, arsenic, made the tenth unique "substance" to be placed at his free-designing disposal. Modern chemistry had not yet developed, and the discovery of "arsenic" was probably an accident of an alchemist's trick.

The year 1250 was also the approximate beginning of modern mathematics, which were self-started out of the introduction into Mediterranean civilization at that time of the cypher (brought from the East by the Arabs). The cypher made possible the positioning of numbers and thereby all modern "cyphering," as "calculation" in general became known. As a result of the calculating facility, the conceptions and assumptions of scientists in general could be translated from a mystical belief to demonstrable and usable reality.

Since that first "isolation" by an alchemist in pre-modern chemistry days, all the rest of the ninety-two chemical elements have been discovered. The chart records the years of those isolations.

Culmination of this set of events put man in command of the complete inventory of building components with which the universe is structured.

This historical portrait has not been painted before. It has not even been familiar to the scientist[1] (he has been pre-occupied with the deeds themselves), so it is not surprising that the historical portrait has not been familiar to the layman. Man's notions of history are identified with a different set of events—the names and places of those persons and events whose political fate (or public relations experts) put them most prominently upon traditional records.

A few of these traditionally documented events have been included in the portrait painted by this chart. They have been included in order to fit the popular picture of history together with this chronological curve of fundamental history. For the identification we have selected those moments when humans could demonstrate their relatively high command over major difficulties of environment by achieving ever-accelerating, world-around travel: first in wooden sailing ships circa 1520, taking two years; second in steel steamships, 1880, taking two months; third in aluminum airplanes, 1945, taking two days; and fourth rocketed in exotic alloy capsules, 1960, taking two hours. How comparatively recent these events of man's space and time mastery are and how relatively short-lived was the supremacy of each as a planetary girdler!

It is to be noted how late, relative to the timetable of arrival of the chemical elements, did the commercial production of steel occur, and that this production came only as a result of

[1] The writer presented this chart for inspection at a luncheon of leading scientists at the Cosmos Club in Washington, D.C., in 1943, and they expressed their unanimous surprise at the picture.

the multi-alloying of the previously isolated chemical elements. The industrial era was built then not on the coming of steel, but on the isolating and harnessing of the elements of which steel was comprised—atoms that compound so densely in dynamic orbiting as to appear superficially "solid." It is the dynamic orbiting of the atoms which provides the special and advantageous behavior characteristics whose high tensile cohesiveness we identify as steel.

It is also to be noted how sequitur to these primary and secondary events of chemical isolation and subsequent admixture are the development of radio and automobile and all those other highly complex technical facilities with whose advent we usually identify the inception of our modern industrial world.

### The Chart as an Instrument of Prognostication

Away from home, on sea or in the sky, the individual has insured his security of tomorrow by the science of navigation. The ability to locate the position of one's ship or airplane on the map is the first function of navigation. Navigation then goes on to plot a corrected position and a new course from the discovered location to the next geographical objective. It is obvious that the fate of ships and planes is based upon employment of these simple principles of observational location and mathematical forecasting. Essential to navigation away from home is the cosmic frame of reference—celestial navigation—which fixes position for and upon Earth, Inc., by reference to Earth's gyrations in the big-league playing field dominated by the Sun and other stars.

In domestic affairs, however, man has not been prone to regard his private and his social and economic activities as ne-

6

cessitous of employing precise navigational principles—certainly not the "cosmic" principles. He isn't "going" anywhere at home. True, he has budgeted his income, which might be considered, poetically speaking, as "navigation" from a known position to a desired objective. True, he does schedule his daily domestic course of affairs by the pre-Copernican "rising" and "setting" of the sun. However, geographically and socially speaking, he assumes that when at home he knows precisely where he is. "Fixing man's position in history might be interesting to the anthropologist or other professors, but not to me," he says. "I'm in a hurry to go nowhere—have to run along now to the ball game."

In social navigation the first phase, i.e. getting a fix, might be said to be provided by history, but history is pretty well packaged in the popular mind as a romantic and unreal appendage of the limited sensation of "here and now."

As for the second phase of navigation, forecasts are also pretty well packaged in the popular mind. They are packaged even less attractively than history—as the questionable trickery of soothsayers, fanatics and comic-strip artists. Of course, the children look forward to growing up in the "here and now"—to long pants, to beaux, to going to college, getting married, having a home of their own, etc., but these are all extensions of exploitation of sensational "self."

Thus egotistically preoccupied, it is a matter only of days before wars that people come suddenly to realization of a great active and seemingly inevitable disruption of the "here and now"—disruptions as final as they are cataclysmic. They were unforeseen because the affairs of man on Earth were not viewed as pursuing an active and scientifically predictable course.

These are generalizations and they apply primarily to the home events of everyday life. Of course we recognize that the

7

most sincere and honored among men prognosticate—as, for instance, most precisely in celestial events, viz., the return of comets in seventy years and the precession of the Earth in millennium cycles. Meteorological experts ever more promptly, accurately and comprehensively appraise world-wide phenomena, forecasting weather for days and even weeks with increasing and well-deserved popular credit of their science and art. In view of these commonplaces of prediction regarding enormous cosmic behavior, it is amazing that man is amazed at his very much less amazing success with directed missiles, both rocket and hurled variety. As minuscule cosmic entities, they are governed by the identical factors that govern the planetary motions. All that man had to do to accomplish this meager success was to set earnestly to measurement of the behavior of the cosmic forces which integrate to describe the trajectories or paths, and thereby to value the relevant factors together in desirable proportions.

The only truly amazing fact is that man's intellectual inertia is such as to frustrate him in attacking the problem of self-navigation due to the impressiveness of his bewilderment by the immediate complexity of self, a complexity far less bewildering than that of the Sun's behavior, which behavior he coolly observes and measures in his scientific establishments and yet holds in such popular disdain in his "realistic" affairs.

In the realm of men's economic and social affairs, it is almost to no avail that statisticians present close-up diagrams of the rising and falling of costs, prices, employment and all manner of special relationships under special conditions and leave it to the reader to predict for himself. Man distrusts these data, knowing that they incorporate too many man-invented factors. On the other hand, attempting to exploit popular credit of celestial prediction, some economists foretell "market" behavior by correlation of panics with sun spots—

but only as convincingly, however, as the ancient wizards, for the phenomena are as scientifically remote as is the delirium within the alcoholic ward on New York's East River from the rising and falling of the ocean's tides within that strait.

Scientific factoring of man's affairs by military and economic strategists of sovereign empires has probably, and long since, evolved secret projections of world affairs with considerable skill. Rarely, however, is this form of scientific prognostication submitted to popular democratic consideration. Seemingly, most statecraftsmen have hitherto assumed that shaping of future events hinged upon power balances and advantages to be gained only by secret strategy and surprise actions. In the operational theory of absolute monarchies, or proletarian dictatorships, such time schedules of action in realization of world empire ambitions must obviously remain secret. In the theory of democracy, however, the time schedules and strategic arguments therefore must be arrived at openly, by published data and broadcast debate.

A cosmic reference chart is obviously necessary for realistic development of popular navigation abilities along the course of economic and social evolution.

Despite many ingenious attempts, there is as yet no comprehensive and absolute historical yardstick-chart maintained by popular credit and volition for everyday reference of events (in a manner similar to popular reference to globes and calendars) and upon which the course of man's development may be plotted, and along which the exact location of his growth at any given time may be identified. If realized, such a chart would reveal a curve of performance events which document incontrovertibly the present fix on overall course, leading from the remote past to the remote future. The course must thereafter be subject to progressive correction by an ob-

9

jective test which measures the effectiveness of discipline of man's acts by admonitions of his intellect.

Popular today are certain charts which record successive military and political events of history and the prevalent legends regarding man's doings of the past. But these are not convincing. People are familiar with the myriad of inaccuracies perverting the popular account of their own day. They know how frequently the daily news identifies inadequately or inaccurately the true causes of events. People therefore reason that history must perforce have amplified these myriad errors of daily record. It becomes reasonable popular speculation that history must be characterized by explanatory legends importantly remote from true facts of cause, effect and personnel. Therefore, it must become popular conviction that the charts of historical reference to popularized items are often romantic fiction.

That there is an insatiable popular desire for an overall historical perspective is well documented by the enormous and continuing sale of Bibles, World Almanacs, encyclopedias, and works such as H. G. Wells's *Outline of History*. That the popular desire for true historical perspective has never been cogently satisfied is explained by the fact that the ability to comprehend the events of history even by science has been precluded hitherto through inadequacy of relevant data.

As a result, we have coddled our "realists'" retention of the thought habit of Earth as the immovable center of the Universe. We have coddled the scientifically untenable concepts of matter as static "things." We speak of the chemical elements as materials. We think of "metals" as static absolutes rather than as subvisible dynamic systems. We have vacillated in adjusting our practical thinking to synchronization with the infinite motion of systematic processes of the all-dynamic Universe in which we must survive. The viewpoint of scholastic

10

administration and lay intelligence has alike been static despite its dynamic intentions and promises.

In the great fundamental change that has come about in the academic world within the last generation, man has come to realize and teach, with a sense of increasing expediency, that his Universe is entirely and ceaselessly in motion, i.e., that all is in motion, submicroscopically or superoptically, if not visibly to the naked eye. A sense of reality of this has been brought home to the individual in his own constantly increasing motion and scope of geographical concern. This sense of urgency and increasing realization on the part of the individual has finally come home, so to speak, through accomplishment of atomic fission and planetary rockets. Popular science magazines are trying to tell the individual that Mr. Einstein's startling and esoteric theories of a quarter of a century ago are now every man's concern, but few men as yet comprehend the how and why of that fact.

However, this can be said of Mr. Einstein to the average individual; that he predicated all his calculations on a far more satisfactory absolute than that employed, for instance, by the federal banking system. The banking system secured its funds by the "conservative" assumption that the Earth and its land is a static and absolute affair and that the tie-down of man to certain limited portions of that land is a certain and highly predictable matter, and that risks predicated on that association could be taken over a period of ten, twenty, and even one hundred years.

Mr. Einstein found that such static assumptions were unsatisfactory and anything but conservative in the development of celestial observations and calculations. He needed an absolute measurement to which he could relate all other measurements of an energized and motion-full Universe. He therefore chose speed as an absolute, the completely unfettered speed

11

of the energy omnidirectionally radiant in a vacuum, which rate of radiant wave growth, $c^2$, had been verified by science's measurement of radiation as visible daylight, infra-red radiation, ultra-violet radiation, and the radiation of radio, all of which had been discovered to have apparently the same speed. Einstein's absolute of cosmic behavior reference is then one of energy articulated as omnidirectionally radiant *speed,* whereas the absolute norm of our present economic accounting is one of absolute rest, absolute static, death, real property, earth-to-earth, mort-gage, the measure-of-death, "man is designed to be a failure," must prove himself an exception, must "earn his living." We misconstrue to be *"at rest"* the land and many objects of our local scenery which are spinning coincidentally at hundreds of miles an hour around our mutual planetary axis as simultaneously our sceneried planet and its Moon co-orbit the Sun at sixty thousand miles an hour, as all the while our star Sun's system and the billion other star systems of our Galaxy co-merry-go-rounding at a peripheral speed of one million miles an hour, all of which is the antithesis of *"at rest."* The inexorable workings of evolution must constantly reinter-position and transform all the only momentarily coincident relationships, which like the hands of the clock seem illusion-arily to be in "natural repose." If the electromagnetic absolute does not supersede the static norm in popular economics, there soon may be no live humans aboard our tiny planet Earth. All the physical organisms accommodating the mysterious weightless phenomenon life aboard planet Earth are meta-bolically regenerated only by star energy radioed to us. Cosmic life support is not operated cash on delivery.

Implicit in Mr. Einstein's successful adoption for celestial science of a comprehensive yardstick of absolute speed is an absolute norm of economic success predicated upon man's historical growth from a past of infinite ignorance of Universe toward a future of infinite knowledge founded quite simply upon the quick realities rather than upon the dead superstitions. This involves measurement of man's transition from his ignorant fixation upon a limited and static association with a little "flat" spot of Earth to his progressive awareness, measurement, and mastery not only of the ocean's and atmosphere's simple and slow motions about the surface of the Earth, but to man's increasing speed relationships to the geography not only of his Earth but to the geography of his technical knowledge.

Although man has as yet employed only minor areas of absolute speed his trend is toward ever increasing mastery of the affairs of energy as absolute speed or, as the latter is interpolated by the Einstein precedent, into relative potential energy shuntings.

Reviewing then: such a curve (to be employed for politico-economic navigation) would identify any point in man's affairs upon the accelerating curve of transition from the limbo of absolute ignorance of Universe toward (and only toward) absolute knowledge and metaphysical mastery of the physical Universe identified by Einstein as absolute energy—"E."

With no misconceptions as to its present shortcomings and its ultimate discard by virtue of a more precise development, the chart which is the subject of this discourse has been developed to take advantage of the assumption that man's present affairs might not only be identified in the great overall history, but a reasonably successful navigational course might be set by which he could progress from the present "fix" of politico-economic position to a position synchronized with the forecast "fix" of tomorrow along the great circle course of transition from absolute ignorance to absolute technical knowledge. Such navigation would not presume to say that man could arbitrarily detour and take a position somewhere "off" the great overall course of history. Such navigation could, however, arrange for man to arrive at tomorrow's fix without the characteristic catastrophes of his past history, as hitherto caused by his ignorance of the inevitability of his arrival at tomorrow's predeterminable technical position.

Tiny as man is, he rarely has the opportunity to identify his measurable stature in history. However, a degree of such awareness is central to the sensations he receives when, for instance, viewing the Grand Canyon for the first time, he looks one mile down and one hundred miles across to the next mountain and sees at once the still-continuing work of millions of years carved by the live river glinting far below.

Inspection of this chart and prospect of this significance can be resolved to a picture of mankind standing on a little sandy strand beside the course of a turbulent river at the bottom of a great canyon. The waters are rising and are certain to rise constantly, eventually to eliminate the tiny strand upon which man had historically existed, a "complete" history of insignificant duration relative to celestial history. It is therefore not a question of whether man chooses to draw pictures in the sand or to dream of building sand houses—it is a question of how he is to stay afloat, if at all, on the roaring stream which will soon seize him in its coursing and how he may possibly attain not only dynamic equilibrium but even—and not unthinkably—a satisfactory life afloat on that course, or upon the seas to which it eventually flows.

The subject chart has been designed to provide some such sensation in man, to provide a positive rather than a negative viewpoint. Rather than being calculated to create a sense of helplessness in the individual, the chart is designed to give him at once a sense of the absolute, irrevocable course of man secured by the phenomenon intellect itself, as separated out from all the minor digressions of man's romantic and inert

14

proclivities. To do this it develops a chronological sequence of events which represent the progressive emergence within the conscious intellect of the absolute principles of nature. The absolute principles may be defined as those measured and logged discoveries of the ceaselessly inquiring intellect into the infinite behavior characteristics of the Universe—the behavior that always was and always will be.

By technical marriage of two or more absolute behavior characteristics man can produce information effects of special advantage at special moments in history—these special effects we call invention. By charting only the special set of absolute principles which comprise this chart and keying that history of dynamic principles to a few events which man has hitherto considered of eminence, the new perspective upon this great curve of transition from absolute ignorance of deathly rest to absolute knowledge of all-quick life, the degree of humanity's self-validation and relative mastery of his ever swifter synchronization with the absolutely swift course may be attained.

## Significance in the Rate of Man's Acquisition of the 92 Element Controls

Technology represents philosophy resolved to the most cogent argument . . . If man did this, such would result. In technology man is empowered to explore and develop his own "if" without reference to the limiting response of other preoccupied egos. Through technology alone the creative individual can of free will arrange for the continuing preservation of mankind despite individual man's self-frustrating propensities. Mechanisms are the antithesis of the Frankenstein concept. They represent the direct and only means of articulation of free will. Mechanisms can only be operated by man.

15

The ultimate economic emancipation of man, potential in the principles of technology, was envisioned by Leonardo da Vinci, who demonstrated to his feudal patron many an augmentation of man's innate faculties of perception, articulation and muscle power. But despite the purity of the principles employed, the augmentations were of low magnitude. This was due to the relative impurity of the materials and energy control technics as yet established in the historical environment in which Leonardo's tangible life occurred. The degree of ineffectuality in that technical environment may be read on the chart in terms of the limited number of elements then recognized, isolated and controlled—only eleven out of ninety-two.

Broad realization of the benefits of elective mechanical extension by individuals of the whole human family had to wait upon the discovery, separation, isolation, behavior measurement and resulting technical control of the complete family of ninety-two chemical elements.

That this attainment in 1932 is epochal can be appreciated only when it is clearly understood that for reasons of mathematical and physical principle, there can be only ninety-two elementary atoms, or unique and independent, as well as dynamically symmetrical, nuclear systems in the geometry of the Universe. The ninety-two elements constitute a finite system, in the same way that a circle constitutes a finite system in contradistinction to a line, whose ends are randomly infinite. The entire behavior "stuff" of our physical Universe is comprised only of these ninety-two regenerative elementary systems or parts or compounds or derivatives thereof.

These "elements" must always be thought of kinetically—as a ninety-two-ring circus so to speak, in which the performance is so microscopically interwoven as to provide not even standing room and therefore to present an optical illusion of solidarity or homogeneity, which is carelessly interpreted as a static "thing."

All in physical Universe is represented by some arrangement, or temporary derangement, of the unique primary behavior roles of the elemental circuses. Figuratively speaking, the new super atoms, those numbered above ninety-two, viz., neptunium, plutonium, curium and americium, are split-second twist-openings of negative Universe.

The ninety-two basic elements represent the full array of simple principles by which energy may impound itself (by angular refraction) like a self-rolling-up ball of string. The new radioactive super atoms may be likened to swiftly unwinding asymmetrical balls. And the radioactive isotopes of the ninety-two basic elements are also in behavior like raveled balls which must be unwound for symmetric rewinding.

If man is to demonstrate any important control of his Universe by his own free will, then all the fundamental behavior phenomena of his dynamic Universe, as demonstrated in the ninety-two primary team plays, must be involved directly or indirectly in the process. To progressively control the Universe, humanity must of necessity first master the behavior of all its parts. Therefore, each and all the principles of energy behavior demonstrated in the atomic system, or as multiplied astronomically in the heavenly systems, will eventually be employed by the intellect in developing the structures, instruments, tools, engines and networks adequate to cope with the magnitudes of heat and stress of this universally available energy with which he will be progressively furnished.

Man's mastery of the energy Universe will be evidenced as progressive conversion of seeming chaos of the total environment into progressively greater ranges of predictable control of his affairs, both time- and space-wise. In this conversion history, 1932 is outstanding. Hiroshima, Bikini and controlled interplanetary vehicles are but bubbles arising in the early wake of this enormous 1932 event of inventory completion, signaling phase two in the great cosmic experiment of intellect articulate in man.

Translating from the principles of nuclear dynamics of the ninety-two elements into economic terms, this progressive mastery will be realized economically by man as a delimiting of the expression of his common wealth, potential or actual. Lasting weal can only be common and common wealth may be defined as the industrially organized ability to project certain and constantly improving standards of survival and moral behavior by the multiplying many without deprivation of any.

However, as we exist here in what we mystically identify as 1947 in the calendar of all-time history, man continues his preoccupation with economic tactics now obsoleted by science. These tactics are predicated upon centuries of fear-generated tradition. The traditions were slowly inoculated by perennial disasters accruing to natural scarcities of the involuntary geographical isolations of premechanized society.

These fixations upon the non-industrialized past blind man's reasoning faculties to the truth, that the greatest revolution in history has been accomplished, and that it is physically practical this minute for the first time in history for men to set themselves methodically to the task of unlimited production for all without invoking a further day of fundamental negative reckoning.

This is because the real costs have been discharged in advance through enormous investments of time, discipline and integrity by the pioneers of intellect. It will take a bit of mental digging by society and a whole lot more disaster to unearth this fact, but that it is fact is precisely what the chart says.

Such a thought would have been preposterous in the days of Columbus or Newton; nonsense in Lincoln's day or even in

18

Wilson's. But as the chart shows, it became true in 1932 with the ninety-second elemental isolation. This last basic isolation coincides with the greatest historical revolution in academic thought. As Irving Langmuir stated, "It was in 1932 that the formal body of science throughout the world acknowledged the concept of universal physical motion." Politically this intellectual revolution coincided with the end of President Hoover's U.S.A. administration. He and the successor political administrators have been tossed as by an earthquake with no traditional precedent evidenced to guide them in the upheaval. Pre-1932 political and economical precedent is now as useless as a book of etiquette in an atomic bomb explosion.

It will take decades to develop popular awareness and political action resulting upon the insistent truth of this revolution. It will take centuries to pull out the last stump roots of fear.


## Preventative Pathology

*Distinction Between Events of Pure Science and Technical Invention; War Unnecessary to Progress*

Despite theoretical knowledge and popular purchase of world globes, "practical" world thought as yet "sees" a flat earth extending motionless about the individual and the "world" standing still in the center of the Universe. Its Sun continues to rise and set. But the horizons of the egocentricity which formerly insulated the maintenance of this erroneous "practicality" are fast vanishing.

The old horizons are evaporating in the light of enormous events of energy articulation, now thought of mostly as embodied in an ominous future or a recent meddling by science. But in fact the events were wholly developed in the past. The real past, as depicted by the chart, was hitherto invisible to the egocentric preoccupations with the "practical" fictions of civilization. Now the fear preoccupation is epitomized in shuddering fascination with the atomic weapon.

The chart of element conquest was devised to accelerate popular awareness of the possibly hopeful significance of the crisis in history now confronting man. Though it attempts to encompass a cogent degree of completeness in the aspects of this truth, while maintaining a comic-strip lucidity, it fails in this respect if the words are not read. Few will take the precious time to read; therefore, it can only hope to offer important reward to the diligent student. However, he may relay his personal conviction of the inherent significance of the crisis to larger numbers of students.

The chart provides a hindsight perspective of the epochal abruptness in the rate of civilizations' measured acquisition of technical knowledge concerning the comprehensive inventory of cosmic absolutes.

It seems to demonstrate that periods of industrial activity in technical syntheses of principles, data, free energy and energy as "matter," find highest employment by the fear-amassed credits of warfare. Therefore the assumption approaches fact that war promotes the major technical advances of civilization. Funded by unprecedented war credits, industrial technology brings into popular use and ways of thought the relative advances in control over universal units of time, space, weight, mass and energy. What has not been clear is that the potential of this emergency-born technology has always accrued to human's prewar individual initiatives taken in a humble but irrepressible progression of assumptions, measurements, deductions, and codifications of pure science.

More broadly stated, warfare itself represents man's postponed, unplanned and violent readjustment of the economic balance sheet to include the cumulative augmentation of his relative mastery of the physical Universe irrevocably established to his credit by the phenomenon intellect, through the interim activities of pure science.

Technological gain is then sequitur to war, but war in turn is sequitur to the events of pure science, which reshuffle the aces of war-power making and inspire the "outs" to rechallenge the "ins."

Inventions are extemporaneous. They represent trial balances of immediate resource and principle drawn off in the light of shifting needs. Inventions are always imperfect and always become obsolete or may never be realized. Unlike inventions, pure science events are absolute and irrevocable.

Pure science events represent openings of windows through the wall of ignorance and fiction, to reveal the only reality— the behavior of the naked Universe that always was, is, and will be. True it is that the first glimpses may be hazy and imperfect, but the behavior itself is absolute and is progressively clarified. Therefore, this comprehensive curve of the chronological rate of acquisition of knowledge concerning the pure science absolutes, separated out from all other events of history, may be inspected as the basic means of prediction of inherent technical and social events—immediate or somewhat distant.

The absolute quality of these causal events of pure science precludes their nonsensical exploitation. Their usefulness to man cannot be inaugurated by downward adjustment of their unlimited advantages. They cannot be fitted directly into the minutely circumscribed traditional life of the individual.

Their inherent benefit can be acquired by man only through direct world-wide referendum. By such referendum the world must adopt a fearlessly willed, new overall objective of civilization. Irrespective of how such a referendum is to take place, this new objective must embody a universal conviction superior to that now held supreme by all political creeds of the world. Ultimate war is as yet the supreme assumption to which all political policy and subsidy-making are ignorantly referenced. Ultimate war paces all politically or possessively biased exploitation of technology.

War represents the uniformed hospital and operating room phase of an only remedial pathology in treatment of man's affairs. In this inherited scheme of life, science and technology are invoked directly by society only at the eleventh hour to arrest the malady fostered by laissez faire, ignorance, opinion, shortsightedness, prejudice and egocentricity. Formally declared war is the final spectacular and open chapter following the prolonged and far more sanguinary private and non-spectacular chapters of strife accomplished under guise of "Peace."

A universal conviction obviously superior to that of inevitable war would be one which assumes as mandatory a preventative pathology in treating with all of man's affairs. *Ipso facto* this is a technical rather than a political scheme. Therefore the referendum cannot be initiated by politics. Political referendums have become negative referendums in which the lesser antipathy is registered. However, our industrial consumer referendum, which is proposed here, can and will be ultimately recognized and incorporated by politics as mandatory. Initiation of the referendum can be accomplished only by the inauguration of a transcendental world-girdling service industry.

### Spontaneous Mass Use: The Absolute Economic Referendum

Patronage of service industry by world peoples will constitute a spontaneous and fundamental referendum. People, however, cannot demonstrate their preference without progressive competitive submissions. New industry can only be initiated by free will. While empirical science works equally well under private or public subsidy, new industry is the pure product of free initiative, imagination and personal risk of the individual, or small groups of individuals, in tendering new service to the industrial referendum.

The transcendental and world-girdling industry which will provide the spontaneous referendum of concurrent popular employment and patronage will belittle all earlier phases of industry and politics. The new universal preoccupation will provide endless employment and wealth of security by mass producing and world distributing geographically unlimited scientific living facilities and their concomitant ever improving services. This transcendental industry will embody direct and comprehensive application to man's personal needs and delights of the gamut of technical advantages already accrued and yet accruing to the tireless intellect.

Initiation of such a transcendental industry motivated the concept of mass production of scientifically prototyped houses. This industry is today the number one responsibility of free enterprise. It will ultimately justify individual enterprise to a world which eyes socialism as its panacea. Only individual enterprise risk can convert scarcity to socializable plenty.

What is predicted here as implicit to the real history demonstrated by the chart is: transition by world society from an overall remedial to a preventative pathology. This is to be accomplished by the self-discipline of individuals through successive gains, first in science; second, in pioneering enterprise; third, in technology; and fourth, in industrial servicing. And the productive results of this evolution of initiative will finally be acknowledged as popularly self-evident and codified as politically desirable and socializable, but only after the fact of individual enterprise.

| 1250 A.D. | 1290 | 1330 | 1370 | 1410 | 1450 | 1490 | 1530 | 1570 | 1610 | 1650 |

SAILING SHIP

EARTH ORBIT IN MAN MADE ENVIRONMENT CONTROL:
PRODUCT OF SUCCESSFUL APPLICATION OF HIGH PERFORM-
ANCE PER UNIT OF INVESTED RESOURCES

PROFILE OF THE INDUSTRIAL REVOLUTION AS
EXPOSED BY THE CHRONOLOGICAL RATE OF
ACQUISITION OF THE BASIC INVENTORY OF COSMIC
ABSOLUTES—THE 92 ELEMENTS

ALGORISMA INTRODUCES CYPHER INTO EUROPEAN CIVILIZATION FROM
ARABS, THUS PROVIDING SCIENCE WITH PRACTICAL CALCULATING FACILITY

LEONARDO DA VINCI
COLUMBUS
COPERNICUS

GALILEO

BO

9 ELEMENTS were acquired
by civilization prior to his-
toric record of the events,
probably in Asia millenniums
ago.

CARBON   #6  C
LEAD     #82 Pb
TIN      #50 Sn
MERCURY  #80 Hg
SILVER   #47 Ag
COPPER   #29 Cu
SULPHUR  #16 S
GOLD     #79 Au
IRON     #26 Fe

10 ARSENIC  #33 As (First recorded discovery) Bavarian    11 ANTIMONY  #51 ·Sb German

9
8
7
6
5
4
3
2
1

APPROXIMATE CUMULATIVE

150

| 1250 A.D. | 1290 | 1330 | 1370 | 1410 | 1450 | 1490 | 1530 | 1570 | 1610 | 1650 |

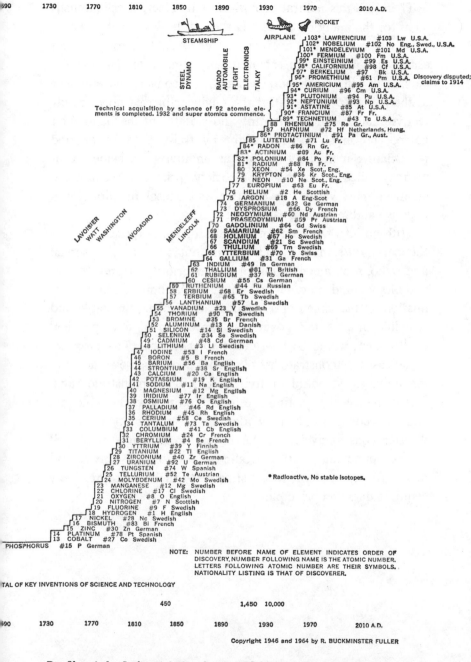

*Profile of the Industrial Revolution, 1946 (subsequently up-dated).*

Therefore this natural evolution of intellectual accomplishment for the many by the few is the antithesis of such reverse-gear schemes as Technocracy, which sought to establish an autocracy of engineers schematically similar to national socialism in aim. Technocracy sought to convert the engineer to the role of politician. But the engineer proved no more effective than the most ignorant and slothful in the ballot box game, and much too forthright by training to be a good politician. Superficially salable as an inviting scheme Technocracy failed as an "out" for society, primarily because the engineer must vacate his creative and causal function for a negative and restraining function.

With no intent to be dogmatic but for the purposes of hypothetical discussion, it is pointed out that by employing screen and radio, such a conviction of the superiority of preventative pathology could be quickly lighted in the human mind. Submission on the screen of a scientifically evolved timetable and schedule of priorities governing conversion of total physical environment would be heartening to the world. The program could easily demonstrate how it would provide an ever advancing universal standard of living. It could demonstrate satisfactory means of adjusting the individual to a world deployed, and to security attained by alert poise and ability to dodge disaster constructively. To be cogent to an eager public, it must be punctuated with periodic or milestone objectives, and means for intermittent readjustments to include progressively acquired data and principle.

# THE LEONARDO TYPE

# THE LEONARDO TYPE

Before the pictorially graphic record of the presence of humanity aboard our planet began there was no way for men to record their individual feelings and thoughts except as manifest in their tool inventing. Words are tools but their sounds could not be made to last, under early history's conditions. Individually identifiable humans had no line of communication reaching directly to us today, other than the evidence of humanity's massive group work in carving, moving, shaping, and building with stones plus the non-identifiable individual's profuse handicrafting of small artifacts such as vessels, arrowheads, beads, etc.

But from the beginning of the pictorially recorded history, on walls, vases, jewelry, et. al., we gain more and more information regarding general human experiences, capabilities, thoughts, and motivation. For instance it is evidenced that throughout all earlier times until yesterday the ruling social powers assumed the human masses to be universally ignorant and accredited them with having only muscle and dexterity value. The illiteracy of the masses was mistakenly interpreted as meaning that the commoner was inherently lacking in intellect—just a "poor wretch."

As "the exception that proved the rule," once in a rare

29

while, by command of some god, a commoner apparently was endowed with creative powers and insights. The ease with which the erroneous assumption could be made that the masses are *stupid* is manifest when we realize how easily a human of today conditioned to speak only americanese could deceive himself into mistaking for an "inherently illiterate Mongol" some ill-clothed, war-bruised, Chinese communist, Ph.D. physicist who had not learned to speak americanese.

During only the last few decades of the two million years within which humans now are known to have been living aboard our planet Earth have the behavioral clues been multiplying sufficiently to suggest that all humans, including the "spastics" et al., are born with a far more comprehensive and superb inventory of subjectively apprehending and synergetically comprehending faculties—as well as objectively articulating capabilities—than has as yet been formally acknowledged to be the case by the present educational establishments' capability-accrediting boards—much less by the politico-social pressure groups such as veterans' organizations or the parent-teacher associations. We may soon discover that all babies are born geniuses and only become de-geniused by the erosive effects of unthinkingly maintained false assumptions of the grownups regarding their conventional ways of "bringing up" and "educating" their young.

It is possible to identify some of the known faculties which we generally assume to be coordinate in those whom society does concede to be adult geniuses. The publicly accredited characteristics of genius consist for instance of an actively self-attended *intuition* opening the conceptual doors for *innate, frequently and combiningly employed, scientific, artistic, philosophical, idealistic, sensorially conceptive, physically talented, logical, farsighted, imaginative,* and *practical* articulations.

30

Leonardo da Vinci, who fortunately avoided the genius-eroding processes, manifested and coordinatingly employed all and more of such conceptual faculties and articulative capabilities. In the graphically recorded history of the last eight millenniums, as well as in the dim twilight of pre-Indo Chinese, Mesopotamian, Egyptian, South and Central American graphic documentations of history, individuals appeared from time to time who grew to maturity without losing the full inventory of their innate, intuitive, and spontaneously coordinate faculties and therewith inaugurated new eras of physical environmental transformation so important as in due course to affect the lives of all ensuing humanity. We will go on to speak of such comprehensively effective but largely unidentified articulators as the *Leonardo type individuals*.

Since the dawning of the most meagerly revealed human history there have been *ten* importantly distinct periods of historical transformations of both the physical and cosmological environments of society. In each of these the environment-reorganizing Leonardo types manifestly have played the leading roles. There are two discernible periods of history as yet to come. We will deal with all twelve.

To each of us *environment* means: *Everything that is not me*. Environment is subdivisible into two parts, physical and metaphysical. The metaphysical environment consists of human thoughts, generalized principles, and customs. The Leonardo types seem to have avoided attempting to reform the metaphysical environment. They are documented only by their employment of the metaphysically generalized principles to reorganize the *physical* constituents of the scenery, apparently assuming intuitively that a more man-favoring rearrangement of the environment would be conducive to humanity's spontaneous self-realization of its higher potentials. Human travelers coming to a river and finding a bridge across it spon-

31

taneously use the bridge instead of hazarding themselves in the torrents.

Physiology and biology make it clear that at the outset of graphically recorded history a universally illiterate, but also probably *not* unintelligent, humanity was endowed with innate and spontaneously self-regenerative drives of hunger, thirst, and species regeneration. The a priori, chemical, electromagnetic, atomistic, genetic, and synergetic designing of these innate drives apparently was instituted by a higher wisdom and formulative capability inherent in Universe than that possessed by any known living man. These drives probably were designed into humans to ensure that human life and its mind —long unacknowledged as highest faculty—ultimately would discover its own significance and would become established and most importantly operative not only aboard planet Earth, but also in respect to the vast, locally evidenced aspects of Universe. *If so,* mind will come not only to demonstrate supremacy over humanity's physical muscle but also to render forevermore utterly innocuous and impotent the muscle-augmented weapons and the latter's ballistic hitting powers. Mind possibly may serve even as the essential, antientropic function of eternally conserving the omni-interaccommodative, non-simultaneous and only partially overlapping, intertransformative, self-regenerating *scenario*—which we speak of as *Universe.*

Mind, operative aboard our planet Earth and probably elsewhere in Universe, in a myriad of effective circumstances, can and may perform the paramount function of conserving the scenario "Universe." If so, it will have to be accomplished by apprehending, comprehending, and teleologically employing the metaphysical, weightless, omni-intercooperative generalized principles of Universe—in strategically *effective degree* and within a critical time limit. This can be accomplished in progressively more effective degree by Earthians competently

32

"fielding" and those physical energy increments, entropically broadcast by the stars, which happen to impinge kinetically upon our Earth as it orbits the Sun. Employing the appropriate biological and physiological principles, these receipts must be collected, sorted, analyzed, synergetically comprehended, and symmetrically combined into complex but orderly, macro- and micro-cohering aggregates and therewith added into the Earth biosphere's resource-conserving and -storing inventory. For it seemingly is manifest that the task of metaphysical intellect is to cooperate with evolution as a major antientropic factor in offsetting the physical Universe's fundamental proclivities of becoming locally ever more dissynchronous, asymmetric, diffuse, multiplyingly expansive, and disorderly.

The kinetic intercomplementarity of finite Universe requires that what disassociates here must associate there. High-pressure atmosphere at one point is balanced by low pressures elsewhere. The stars are all radiantly dissipating energy. The Earth is a celestial center wherein energies from the stars are being collected and buried ever more deeply. When after vast millions of years, enough energy has been impounded aboard our spherical space vehicle Earth—then it will become a radiant star, as the discard of other burnt-out and dissipated stars are concurrently aggregate elsewhere—some trillions of years again to become a star. No factor operative aboard our planet is so effective in aggregating, reorganizing, concentrating, and refining the disorderly resource receipts as is the human mind.


### Period One

We can discern Period *One* of our twelve-period history in the behavioral traceries we have of the ancient seafaring fishermen-farmers of Japan and coastal China, who seem to have learned through experience of the water-borne or earth-rooted vegetation's unique ability to impound the Sun's radiationally delivered energy and likewise of the Sun's on-going regeneration of more vegetation from the seeds of the vegetation's fruits and tubers. They also found that though the Sun energy was impounded in the vegetation, very little of the latter could be eaten by humans. Men could not eat the bark, trunk, stalks, and could eat but few of the leaves. They found out, however, that animals, bugs, worms, and other creatures could eat the vegetation and could discriminate, as man could not, as to which were poisonous and which were safe. Man could most safely eat the live killed flesh of the animals. But the meat could only be kept viable in cold climates. In the tropics men learned by watching the animals, which of the vegetables, berries, etc. were non-toxic and safe for cultivation. As hounds were used to track animal food in the cold countries, the domesticated cattle were used as safe vegetation "hounds" and their females were also milkable. Despite any known later historical events impinging on the freely and safely wandering cattle of India this is probably the most important single factor explaining this spontaneous social behavior. Sun energy was thus converted into viably tender fruits, roots, shoots, seeds, and nuts of safe vegetation or into animal milk or flesh growth and thence as food converted into human *growth*. The human growth was not only in size, but in muscular ability to do further work by investing its available time in rearranging local environmental events and materials to produce ever higher, human-life-extending advantage.

The Universe and the immensity of everything that was not self and the locally permitted independence of action determined by man's will, as altogether manifest in nature, integrated in man's mind to imply a vast but obviously competent, pattern-formulating, a priori, *mysterious greatness* to be operative throughout all of nature which humans referred to singularly or plurally with some voice-sounded word—such as God—or some counterpart of that economically vocalized term of vague but spontaneous acknowledgment of the presence in Universe of a knowledge, wisdom, and power greater than that possessed by self or any other known humans.

Most prominent in God's total kingdom and most understandable of God's major roles was that of God's functioning in the role of the Sun. As the Sun died each evening and was reborn each morning, death was assumed to be only an invisible state and life was eternally regenerative. The natural water- and land-occurring abundance which the ancestors of the Sino-Japanese had the good fortune to find and the life which it permitted seemed good. That the Japanese national flag should thousands of years later be emblazoned as yet with the Sun is testimony of their enduring and fundamental comprehension of the omni-regenerative scheme of the Universe.

These people, from the earliest historically interpretable times, expressed their gratitude to God, who apparently had pre-fashioned the places most suitable for humans to find themselves, all unexpectedly, expressing spontaneous thanksgiving (worship). These places were (and as yet are) unusually beautiful and inspiring places, occurring randomly and unexpectedly around the world, wherein one is surprised to find oneself from time to time. In such "beauty" spots, designated as *fung shui* by the Chinese, men spontaneously tend to feel mysteriously closer to a wisdom and grandeur of conceiving greater than their own. Such places are unexpectedly intimate to the comprehensively acknowledged mystery identified as God. At the threshold point of such secretly beautiful places the Japanese-Chinese fisherfolk mounted the keel of a ship, spanningly, atop two posts as a doorway or gate (the *torii*) through which they stepped into their vast invisibly walled cathedral. Their particular ritualistic way of thanking God, which has persisted through the millenniums to this day, is known to us as the Shinto religion. Their people brought fish, fruit, grain crops, and wine, in sacrificial denial to themselves of its nourishment in support of their own immediate personal wants, and in order to identify specifically to God that for which they were thanking him. When their sacrifice was prepared and displayed on some form of raised prominence (altar-alter: high), one by one they stepped forward and clapped their hands twice loudly to gain God's attention. Then the individual picked a fresh green leaf from a pre-cut tree branch and placed it on the altar. Thus having given thanks the individual clapped his hands twice more to let God know he was through with his message of gratitude—so that God could get back to his great work of operating Universe and within it providing for the regeneration of all life. No mouthed words were spoken and in a universally obvious pre-word language, man said to God that he sensed intuitively the as yet undiscovered photosynthesis to be operative in some mysterious way in the green leaf which was God's invention for transforming and transmitting the life-supporting energy of Sun to man on Earth. Often men's intuitions have identified and superstitiously employed and conserved for centuries, even millenniums, crude, hypothetical concepts regarding phenomena which are critical to the sustenance of life, which concepts were formulated before those humans had made scientific discovery of some of the chemical and physiological details of such processes, as, for instance, that of the photosynthesis accomplished by the green leaf's as yet only vaguely identified chlorophyllic behavior.

As has been shown by Sir James Frazer in his book *The Golden Bough,* the religions of the people around Earth, before the dawn of our eight thousand years of graphically communicated history, seem all to have been founded upon gratitude to God for the mysterious bounty of nature and in profoundly moving awe of the secrets of fertility—which are as yet fundamentally secret, despite man's having identified such genetic mechanisms as DNA and RNA, and their amino and enzymic realizations. Thus has much of human society recently come to be novelty-intoxicated and glib with scientific jargon. But much of Western society is now hung over with a specialization-obscured sense of the whole. Humanity has temporarily lost its spontaneous acknowledgment of a wisdom greater than its own "hepness."

Because society has physiologically discovered a considerable amount of data, it mistakenly assumes that it is only a matter of a few days, months, or years before all humanity will know what "it is all about." World youth, however, is beginning to intuit that this may not be true—either now or forevermore—for fundamental reasons inherent in the experience manifest, synergetically catalyzed, intuition of the a priori existence of an integrity and competence which probably is forever decomposing and recomposing the scenario "Universe."

To those in ancient times who found their prime sustenance in the sea, God was a sea creature, ergo, being God, and logically a magnificently awesome creature, he was imagined to be a colossal sea serpent whose vertically waving back could be seen moving along, and all the way around, the ocean's faraway watery horizon. Later, as men found that they could employ wind to propel their rafts, by mounting spars and sails, God was imagined to be a dragon or the same sea serpent with wings.

Those who found life support exclusively through the god-given abundance on the dry land were of two prime categories: the hunters in the North, where the flesh food could be preserved by ice, and the agrarians of the South, where the fruits, nuts, and tender-leaved grains of rice, oats, wheat, and corn were in abundance and could be dried and stored indefinitely to be later ground, dehydrated, and baked back into viability.

The agrarians imagined their god to be female—to be the fertility goddess—because the new seed always came out of the womb of the old seed's fruit. The hunters and animal milkers tended to imagine their god to be a male, typified by the four-legged king bull of the animal herds roaming on the land. These early people must intuitively have sensed that the pre-procreative battles of the bulls guaranteed the genetic inclusion of the physically strongest strains. The bull identity of the male fertility god as yet inspires the life drives of some of the dwellers along the Arctic coasts. There the whales come annually and their meat, bones, and oil supply the energies necessary for humans to survive in the icy barrenness of the North. Thus the Point Barrow Eskimos of today still think realistically of the bull-whale as being their Big Brother who returns annually to their Arctic waters to ask the Eskimos to kill him expertly and beautifully so that he may be released to return again next year in the familiar and useful form of another bull-whale, again to fertilize the school of female whales.

The people of pre-written history who found ready sustenance and did survive found no need for a walled-in, roofed, and thus deliberately isolated, environment for worship; the whole, visible Universe was their "house of god." They saw the living creatures and plants wither only to be replaced by more fresh life and this amplified their concepts of life as a scheme of eternal self-reproduction. Life was absolute and continuous and, as with the snakes' successive skins and the crabs' shells, only the fleshy vehicles which life employed in its successive manifestations were temporary and expendable. God was the *continuous* Universe.

We have, however, only the carefully perpetuated religious and superstitious customs of those who were successful in those times to inform us of all the foregoing. Almost no records are left to tell us of the philosophy of those multitudes who did not find life successful and perished at an early age. We have only the subconscious, genes-triggered instincts—underlying the spontaneous adaptations to prevailing conditions, plus the spontaneously retaught mores which conditioned postnatal attitudes of the successful tribal survivors, as handed on meticulously by word of mouth and pantomimic dance, from generation to generation—to guide our exploratory thoughts into the graphically undocumented past.

Filmer S. C. Northrop of Yale writes in his book *The Meeting of East and West* of the effects of the eighteenth-century impingement of the cosmological, highly formalized, "Christian" dogma of (European) Spanish invaders upon the people of Mexico, at the midpoint of the North and South (American) continents, to which vast numbers of humans already had come, from Asia across the Pacific and from the Pacific islands, during untold numbers of earlier millenniums. These Pacific basin people whom the Spanish invaders found in Mexico showed a crossbred physiognomy embracing every physical feature and skin color known anywhere around the Earth. They were so crossbred that they could no longer be spontaneously differentiated into separate "color" races. This crossbreeding is most advanced in both Mexico and India today, but now embraces all the European features as well. Every variety of angular pattern variation in physiognomy is

39

found in both countries in every skin color and every shade from intensely dark to intensely light. Hair ranges through every known variety between straight to tight curly, in every hue from black to platinum blond, and all varieties of hair adorn all varieties of skin color in all degrees of shading from dark to light, which in turn adorn all varieties of facial features and head shapes, wherefore few Mexican individuals can be identified as being of any hybrid race. They are simply worldians.

When the Spanish Europeans brought their official religion of Christianity in its most arbitrarily dogmatic form of the Father, Son, Virgin Mary, and the saints to Mexico's worldians, the latter seemingly accepted that latinized catholicism but went on in swift course, impelled by the momentum of their earlier conditioned reflexes to worship only the Virgin Mary, who was obviously not the same lady as that honored by the pope but was indeed their age-old fertility goddess with a new name—Guadalupe.

In a concept approximately identical to the Eskimos' whale conception the earliest known religious lore of the Asian and Asia Minor hunters held that God was a male who reappeared in generation after generation—to eternity—in the form of the king bull and required of the hunter that he, God in the bull, be most skillfully and honorably slain so that God could be released in order that he might reinvest himself anew and reinvigoratingly in the next generation to produce the sustaining bounty of human food. In the same way the bull-god culture of the pre-history hunters came westward by ship through the traditions of the Asia Minor Phoenicians and was transposed to the Cretan Minoans (named for the Minotaur —which was the bull, their god). From Crete, the bull culture again went even farther westward by ship to Spain. Gradually, the ritualistic bull slaying was modified into the splendor of the bullfight. But today the toreador is more esteemed than the bull, for no longer does Spanish society think in the hunters' experience-generated terms which identified God in the bull.

This bull-slaying rationale was fortified in earliest time by the fact that the oft repeated cutting back, or pruning of the life vehicle, frequently improved the growth. The concept of the prince hidden in a frog or larger beast to be released only by its being killed by the perceptively pure princess is a typical fanciful by-product of the earlier Pantheism (Pan-*the*-ism). The linguistic tool known as an article *"the,"* meaning God, is also *the* root content of *the* Greek letter *theta,* omnipresent God. The male and female prefixes of the Latin world occurred because of the admixture of male-female god concepts halfway between the all-male god bull-whales of the animal-hunting North and the all-female goddess of the agrarian South lands. *Pan* means *everywhere,* as in pan-o-ramic. *Pan-the*-istic means *God is always present in every phenomenon.*

In all the pantheistic cosmologies coming over the threshold of pre-history, God, being everything, was also in man as one of God's myriad variety of manifestations. Those who died were not looked upon as gone but simply as invisible, transmigrated, or transformed.

The most prodigiously permanent record of the cosmology of those pantheistically rationalizing people exists today in the mistakenly named "temples" (wats, ghats) of Southeast Asia. For instance, the most recent centuries' wats of Angkor in Cambodia are apparently replicas of earlier edifices. The wats and ghats are schematically conceived cosmological models of humanity's most thoughtful representation of the structure of our world as informed by travelers' tales of the total sensorial perception. These cosmological symbol edifices apparently were designed under the following circumstances and observations.

41

Speaking omni-historically, humanity within any one average life span has seen less than one millionth of the total surface of our spherical spaceship Earth. This holds true from the earliest known humans until the mid-twentieth century. Throughout the vast ages of recorded history, man's locomotion being limited to his, or his animal's, leg-coverable distances on land and by boats at sea, man thought it to be obvious that the world was geometrically a horizontal slab with various aberrations of mountains and valleys superimposed. Thus humans have been spontaneous victims of the illusion that their world is an infinitely vast, watery plane, surmounted centrally by an immense island of dry land. To understand further the cosmological design of these early Southeast Asian edifices, we must recall that artifacts of the seafarers make it clear, today, that ancient man had discovered the North Star as the axis of the easterly rising out of the sea of the Sun and stars, and their westerly splashdown disappearance into the water. Ancient sea people tended to think spontaneously of their world in terms of north, south, east, and west quadrants. Thus came about our as yet prevalent, deep-rooted, cultural reflex expression "The four corners of the Earth." The Khmer civilization's Angkor Wat or Angkor Thom are physical models of that concept of the world. They are vast, square-based, dry-land models completely surrounded by watery lakes or moats. To ensure that the concept of water completely surrounding the land was lastingly incorporated in their cosmological models, when no water was at hand or when the waters evaporated, the architects edged their great square models of the world with a serpentine rail with separate heads at both ends occurring at the entrance of the model. This serpent was "Naga," their sea serpent God of the Sea.

"Everyone who has traveled at all," the ancient pantheists

must have said, "knows that as one goes inland from the sea —everywhere surrounding the four-cornered world—that one comes to ever higher mountains." This implied that if one went far enough inland one would come to a mountain reaching to heaven and therefore occupied at its highest point by God, with lesser gods at lower altitudes. Their living God-King was a member of one of those lower-altitude gods who was residing temporarily at the even lower Earth level where common mortals dwelt. So the pantheists' cosmological model of a "wide-wide," four-cornered world surrounded by the sea is a great edifice consisting of a concentric system of imitation mountains with each more central mountain pinnacle reaching higher toward heaven. Their first such models were constructed of wood which could adequately accommodate their king during his return to a higher position among the gods. But it often happened that one new God-King replaced another within such short intervals that they began to use the same model for successive kings and gradually replaced the wooden parts with stone parts to make them more durable. But the mistake should not be made of thinking of these edifices as having anything to do with ordinary people. They were not houses of worship in any sense.

These cosmological models of a wide-wide, four-cornered planar Earth surrounded by infinitely extensive waters and surmounted by ever higher central "mountain" pinnacles disclose how the early humans explained the sum of their experiences to themselves regarding the structure and operating scheme of their real world, from out of whose eastern watery extremity the Sun and stars rose, passed over, descended, plunged in and through again. Because the Sun and stars quite obviously passed *over*, and returned *under it,* the world was implied to be a thick but penetrable watery slab

43

extending horizontally to infinity in all planar directions. All the perpendiculars to that slab's base plane were mathematically demonstrable as parallel to one another. Those perpendiculars then were extended in only two directions in relation to man's erroneously conceived flat Earth. Those two exactly opposite, positive and negative, exclusively perpendicular directions in respect to the horizontal Earth plane were the seemingly obvious concepts *up* and *down*.

But we now know that we do not live on a flat slab and that we do live on board an eight-thousand-mile-diameter spherical spaceship speeding around the Sun at 60,000 m.p.h., spinning axially as it orbits. None of the perpendiculars to a sphere are parallel to one another. The first aviators flying completely around the Earth within its atmospheric mantle, and cohered to the planet by gravity, having completed half their circuit, did not feel *up* side *down*. They had to employ other words correctly to explain their experiences. So aviators evolved the terms "coming-*in*" for a landing and "going-*out*" not *down* and *up!* Those are the proper directional words *in* and *out*. We can go only *in, out,* and *around*. Anyone spontaneously seeking to prove his "practical" sense who says "never mind that theoretical stuff—LET'S GET DOWN TO EARTH!"—probably banging the table with his fist as he says it, is disclosed as being insane. We must reply to him, *"Where* and *what* is that 'down to Earth' phenomenon?"

All those misconceptions of the long-ago Southeast Asians' cosmological models we find to be deep-rooted in our own twentieth-century self-misinformed "commonsense." Commonsense was assumed by society to be the antithesis of lunacy. It as yet is. But now we know that the lunacy conforms strictly to the cosmological reality and that the "down to Earth" commonsense of yesterday is fundamentally misinformed. Here

44

we discover the basis for the intuitive discrediting of the older generation by world youth who are directly informed by the astronauts as to the nature of celestial reality.

Thus, our exploration of the Southeast Asian edifices of the millenniums-ago Nagas has begun to clarify our present era's great metaphysical revolution. The great edifices of the Central American Mayas and Incas were also the same four-square, cosmological models and were likewise constructed not to be occupied but either to be surmounted or under-passed by man. Thus also did it come about that the earliest Babylonian and subsequent Egyptian pyramids were also square-based and highly formalized, "single" mountain edifices.

No one knows of any specific, individual personalities who discovered and inaugurated the acknowledgment of a greater authority than that of man in the first invisible, abstract God, who designed and built hallowed spaces for thanksgiving, nor does anyone know of any specific individuals who designed those cosmological wats of Southeast Asia, but their inspiration and economic authority was clearly that of a popularly spontaneous acknowledgment of a mandate from the gods to identify the conceptual scheme of the interrelationship of the gods to the world they had created or that had been created possibly by an ever higher god, all of which creative scheme had structural and operative logic consistent with the experience-won information of contemporary humanity. The design authority was probably that of priest-navigators, for the wats are found either near the sea or near to canals or rivers leading to the sea, and the conformation of their structuring, which was at first of wood, employs principles inherited from boatbuilding arts. We find the descendants of the navigator-astronomer-priests of those earlier times reaching weakly even into our times in the Polynesian chieftains' separation of the habitats of the navigators from the tribe, also in the as yet superstitiously heeded astrology. We also have clues of that world around priest-navigators' cosmological authority in the more recent of past centuries' astronomical "observatory" structures as yet standing in India, Mesopotamia, Crete, Egypt, England, and Central America.

In the early dawning of graphically chronicled civilization the wats involve gods of the sea and gods of the sky, as well as gods of the underground land. The fire, smoke, and lava of volcanoes, well known to men, indicated that *down* led through the horizontal plane of the world into a hell of brimstone and fire, just as *up* led everywhere exclusively toward the serene blue heaven of the highest god.

Most importantly to our comprehensive cosmological survey of all history we must remind ourselves repeatedly that these cosmological symbol edifices had no direct personal relationship to humans. They were constructed only for the convenience of the livingly visible God-King's reascension from Earth to become once more an invisible god of heaven, capable of returning at any future time to resume human or any other convenient form. Thus millenniums later, when Buddha became divinely inspirational to man, one generation of priests after another installed statues of Buddha in niches in the old "mountains" of the wats and ghats. But the wats, ghats, et al., as originally constructed, symbolized nothing for the humans other than the existence of gods who according to the priests could be humored by sacrifices to bring about more favorable conditions for the momentarily living God-King. Humans were absolutely expendable, either as slaves or as sacrifices. Thus we close Period One of our *twelve-period world history* which was constructed only inferentially by extending backward the first historically disclosed data. We can surmise that the economic authority patron of the Leonardo type designers of Period One was that of the gods or God-King.

## Period Two

Period *Two* of our overall twelve-period history—ten past and two to come—begins with the first graphically pictured history of world society as recorded in the stone carvings of Egypt, Mesopotamia. At this time humanity at large knew nothing of physics, chemistry, or biology. Humans recognized but few safe edibles. Humans had witnessed many lethal poisonings by superficially attractive items plucked from the mysterious scenery. Infection was rampant. Average survival was in the neighborhood of twenty-two years or about one fourth of the once-in-a-rare-while demonstrated, biblically mentioned "three score and ten" years' life span. Life was so fundamentally awful that no logic could persuade humanity to believe that the living experience was intended by the maker of Universe to be directly *worthwhile* and desirable in its own right. The only tenable assumption was that life on Earth was suffered only in preparation for a life hereafter. It was reasoned that the worse that life on Earth proved to be, the better would be life hereafter. Experience seemed to show that adequate sustenance in general was so fundamentally scarce that even in the hereafter there could be enough only for one.

Thus it came about in Period Two of our twelve-period history that the *economic authority patronage* which employed and subsidized the efforts of the Leonardo type—intuitive artist-scientist, poet, inventor, engineer, and initiator of the

47

early Egyptian eras—was exclusively the *life hereafter of the Pharaoh.*

The economic license to employ whatever capabilities he could visualize as existing in the non-obvious but intellectually conceptual resources hidden in the scenery went to the Leonardo type to support his reorganization of environmental potentials for the advantage of the life hereafter of the Pharaoh and of his most faithful servants.

As with all building there is a scaffolding activity—a "make ready." The Leonardo type existing in the times of the earliest Pharaohs conceived of the principle of levers and of the ability to move great rocks. He recognized that he could vastly augment the muscles of whole armies of slaves. He conceived that these slaves must be fed in order to put out energy. The Leonardo type conceived of the fact that the waters of the Nile could be allowed to flow into man-produced irrigation ditches to be dug by slaves which would lead the Nile into the potentially fertile floodlands bordering the river. Thus the Leonardo type rearranged the environment of the living in preferred ways which increased in ever multiplying degree the technological advantage as well as human resources and their combined ability to rearrange the environment to ever higher energy-producing degree.

When the Pharaoh died and the Leonardo type was rewarded by being entombed with the Pharaoh along with the other most faithful servants so that they could enjoy the blessings of the "hereafter," the irrigation ditch did not obliterate itself nor was the principle of the lever forgotten among the as yet living people. These physical scaffolding capabilities of the pre-afterlife living society persisted and multiplied as one Pharaoh after another was advantaged by the successive Leonardo types of scientists, artists, and environment-comprehending rearrangers all combined in one man.

Finally the "scaffolding equipment" employed in the pre-death days by the living slaves as led by the eras' Leonardo types, became so prodigious that it became manifest that it obviously would be possible not only to organize to maximum degree the advantages not only of the afterlife of the Pharaoh but also to employ the excess environment-mastering capability to accommodate the afterlife of the nobles as well. Thus developed Period Three of our twelve-period history.

## Period Three

During our historical Period *Three* the progressively ever more prodigious rearrangement of the living environment technology, as temporary scaffolding for the eternal afterlife, multiplied to such a degree that it became spontaneously apparent to all concerned that the total of now mastered workable energy capability made possible the accommodation not only of the afterlife of the Pharaoh and of the nobles, but also of middle-class society. This inaugurated Period Four of our twelve-period history as determined by the economic patronage of the Leonardo type artist conceivers.

## Period Four

In Period *Four,* we discover the work of the artists preoccupied with the afterlife enshrinement of the prosperous middle class. Family mausoleums and burial urns abound. Eventually the environment-altering activity of the in-life, temporal scaffolding technology, devised for the exclusive afterlife enjoyment of kings, nobles, and middle class, became so vast that surprisingly new thoughts were inspired and pronounced by several Middle East and Far Eastern prophets such as Buddha, Mohammed, and Christ, which found it logical to assume that there also could be provision for the afterlife not only of the king, nobles, and middle class, but for *all humanity* including the most lowly commoner. Thus was introduced Period Five.

## Period Five

Period *Five* lasts approximately a millennium and one half —the years A.D. 1 to A.D. 1500—unaltered by any new overriding patronage of the Leonardo type activity. Period Five witnesses the anonymous Leonardo types designing the great cathedrals of Europe. The highly organized physical resource capabilities all lead society toward the realization of a divinely satisfactory afterlife even of the most lowly of free men. In Period Four, slaves and indentured servants had been considered to be subhuman, and in Period Five they as yet often were overlooked in the newly oriented considerations of humanity.

Unfortunately holdovers of this viewpoint persisted here and there throughout Period Five. The "subhuman" status of slavery involved unfortunates taken in battle of all colors of skin. Unfortunately for their sake, those who had acquired the darkest skin in multi-generations of environmental adaptivity in the tropical Sun areas had also enjoyed a clothing-free functional body development which produced a physical superiority, and which in turn brought the highest prices paid in the slave markets. For millenniums the majority of prisoners of war who were cast into slavery were predominantly of white or swarthy skin, but their work value was so inferior to that of the black-skinned prisoners that in the great slave markets such as that of Delos the whites and swarthier be-

50

came obsolete as slaves. This reduced the slave ranks to an almost exclusively black variety until, as we shall see in Period Seven of our history, the inanimate power-driven machines made even the blacks obsolete. With the coming of inanimate power-driven tools, the automatons, which are both unpaid slaves and wage slaves, also became obsolete but have not even today been effectively conceded to be so by the lingering mores of an unenlightened, fearful society.

Finally in Period Five, the enormous magnitude of technological development going into the scaffolding preparations for the sublime afterlife, of *all* those classified as humans, proliferated in life to such an extent that society began to realize that not only the afterlife of everyone could be accommodated but also the *living life* of the king.

## Period Six

This opened Period *Six* of our twelve-period total history. Its beginning is identified with the beginning of what became socially recognized as "The Divine Right of Kings." God apparently had ruled that certain individuals should enjoy life itself as well as afterlife.

In Period Six the Leonardo type is patronized by the *living* king as well as by the *life hereafter* of the sovereign, nobles, middle class, commoners, and in most areas even of the slaves, both black and white.

## Period Seven

As the temporal technology proliferated yet further in Period Six, it became evident that humanity could be organized to produce a bounteous *life* for the *nobles,* as well as for the king, while also accommodating the afterlife of all humanity. This inaugurated Period *Seven* of our twelve-period history. This is the period introduced by the Magna Carta. We have the artists making extraordinarily powerful and effective physical devices. Such paraphernalia as tools, weapons, painting, and sculpture were all made by the artists' own hands. All were made to advantage and to please exclusively the living kings and living nobles, as well as the afterlife of all humanity.

## Period Eight

Again the multiplying proliferation of technical capability and material resource availability and investible man-hours of society finally permitted the temporal life advantaging even of the *middle class* and that inaugurated the *Eighth Period* of our ten past and two forward periods of history. Period Eight became what we know as the Victorian Era. It lasted through the Gay Nineties and into the turn of the twentieth century. It terminated with the beginning of World War I in 1914. But as usual, the termination of a period overlapped the beginning of another. Period Nine begins almost unnoticed in the midst of the Gay Nineties.

## Period Nine

With the 1895 invention of the automobile, radio, X ray, and automatic machine tools, and their subsequent twenty-two-year gestation into full-fledged industries, there was clearly established by 1917 the beginning of Period *Nine* of our twelve-period, all-history review of fundamental environmental rearranging followed by social reorientation as inaugurated intuitively, conceptually, and practically by the Leonardo type environment transformers. We had clearly established before the beginning in 1914 of World War I a vastly amplified resource realization by the Leonardo type and especially the newcomer crossbred industrial society Leonardo of the North American continent. These latter-day Leonardo types saw that the total environment had become so effectively rearranged that it made possible the *advantaging* not only of the *afterlives of all humanity* but also now of the *living experience of all humanity*.

At this new juncture the Leonardo types, who had for all the first eight periods been personally producing the prime designs with their own minds and the realization of those designs by the fine crafting of their own hands and exclusively human-muscle-powered tools, comprehended that there were not enough of their own Leonardo type artist-scientists, philosophers, and craftsmen to manufacture, i.e., manu-(hand)-facture(make), i.e., meaning to produce with their own hands, all the physical items that could and must be produced for all of humanity.

It was at this historical twentieth-century dawning moment of Period Nine that the Leonardo type realized that the energies which were being applied to the ends of levers—in the form of water wheels—which were pulley- and belt-connected to general overhead rotating shafts of factories and thence by pulleys and belts to individual machines, to which latter individual, wire-connected electric meters were directly attached—that so much inanimate energy-driven productivity was thus made possible that he must of economic necessity now preoccupy himself with the invention and production of special machine tools and forming dies to be operated from the central power-driven shafting. These tools they saw would in turn *mass-reproduce* the *end products* of their designing for the advantage of all humanity. Thus we enter into the Ninth Period of our history of the economic subsidizing of what is known as the creative, or Leonardo type man, i.e., the *mass production* industry age.

Mass production was first applied to materials for other contractors or manufacturers to use and not for consumer end products. Mass-produced nails went to the carpenter contractor to hammer into the final building. The first direct consumer-distributed mechanical "end products" to be mass-produced were the pocket watches of Ingersoll, and the alarm clocks. Then came Singer's sewing machines and Gillette's razors.

Henry Ford, who thought of "art" as consisting only of Americana, fiddlers, and twinkle dancing, and gave little consideration to the art of other countries and times, thought of his own productive efforts as strictly classifiable only under the heading of prosaic "work," or more specifically, as "hard" mechanics, engineering, and commerce.

Ford was inspired by the needs of the farmer, having himself been born a farm boy. The great mass of humanity at that time continued to be farmers as in the past millenniums. Ford gradually evolved an omni-kinetic electromagnetically powered and intercommunicated network of industrialization and its most effective employment of the world-around, unevenly occurring, geographically remote resources which had to be integrated in order to permit ever higher performance capabilities by metallurgical alloying, precision forming, and synergetics in general.

Henry Ford introduced the era of employment of the 99 percent invisible ranges of the electromagnetic spectrum reality. Man's eye cannot distinguish modular intervals of less than 1/100 of an inch. Ford introduced measurement controls of

1/10,000 of an inch in his automobile-manufacturing technology. He was mistakenly identified as a stubborn old man who persisted in making just one type of black automobile—the Model T. While his General Motors competitors were preoccupied with customer courting by improving primarily only the visible instrument panels, visible upholstery, shift levers, motor hoods, mudguard shaping, and other sensorially pleasing modifications, Henry Ford was inaugurating the mass use of the invisible and ever higher performance per pound alloys and the invisible controls of ever closer measuring of invisibly operating parts of the machinery, structure, and production tooling of his automobiles. He was also the first to mass-produce automobiles on moving assembly lines. Nothing bigger than sewing machines had previously been mass-produced. Ford also concerned himself directly as the prime designer of his evolving machinery and structural technology and all the other supporting activities of final pertinence to the success of the massively reproductive industry. He led the design of his factories, tools, mining, transporting of raw materials all around the world, railroads, ships, loading equipment, communications and information handling systems. Ford was personally and inventively concerned with each and every techno-scientific and economic involvement from the raw resources situated in the scenery to the design and maintenance of the production equipment research evolution and, of course, with the design of the end product automobiles and tractors themselves.

As a consequence of all the foregoing historical initiatives when Henry Ford replaced the Model T with the Model A, he was employing fifty-four different alloys of steel in his Model T. These alloys were as unlike one another as diamonds are unlike pearls. But the electromagnetic, structural arrangements of those alloyed atoms were all invisible. Henry

Ford's establishment for humanity of all these invisible capabilities prevented his cars from suffering the swift deterioration of his competitors' only superficially more *"attractive"* vehicles. Though the farmers were unable to see the alloys and were unaware of their existence, the cars lasted and lasted despite rough usage, with little maintenance, and almost without any weather protection. They had far greater performance per pound, hour, and kilowatt of invested physical resources than had any of the other contemporary vehicles. Most of Henry Ford's one hundred and twenty car-manufacturing competitors of the first quarter of the twentieth century did not last, nor did their cars. But many of those earlier Ford cars as yet exist, particularly his Model A, of 1928, and are as yet demanding good prices, while most of the names of Ford's at one time one hundred and twenty contemporary competitors are almost altogether forgotten and their cars are only to be found in museums.

By the mid-twenty-first century with the perspective advantage of time, it may come to pass that Henry Ford will have become recognized by world-around society as the Leonardo of the twentieth century, for it was Henry Ford, Sr., who first organized the mass production effectiveness of science and technology and its comprehensive logistical revolution as well as evolving the supporting new economics and world mass distribution of the high-performance products of mass production industry whose controls lay exclusively within the realm of the 99 percent invisible physical reality. He was the first to recognize that mass production is impossible without mass consumption and that required much higher wages which Ford was the first to institute. Through the great depression his operation continued as others closed and failed. Henry Ford thus introduced and held the prime initiative for Period Nine of our overall history.

Henry Ford set the stage for *Period Ten* of that part of our overall evolutionary history in which man consciously participates and takes responsibility for the transformations of both the environment and the consequent social behaviors of adjustment to the successively new environments.

## Period Ten

Henry Ford also set the stage for, but did not lead, the inauguration and development of Period *Ten* of our overall transformational history. Period Ten was opened by a century-long succession of masters of the invisible reality—Newton, Hertz, Maxwell, Faraday, Boyle, Avogadro, Mendeleyev, Van't Hoff, Michelson, Planck—and finally secured by Einstein. Ralph Waldo Emerson defined poetry as "saying the most important things in the simplest way." By that definition Einstein became and will probably remain history's greatest poet—for who could say so much so simply as did Einstein when he described physical Universe as $E = Mc^2$?

There are varying time lags in the rate of industrial gestation of the Leonardo type's inventions. The least lag occurs between invention and industrial use in the electronics industry. Here the technical advantages are conceived of and realized only by the invisible, mathematical probing of scientists. The invisible improvements are adopted because their logic can be disclosed only by mathematics. There are no grounds for sensorially based and conditioned reflexive objections: i.e., for exclusively *opinionated* arguments. Inventions in the aeronautical arts and their industrial support field are adopted within five years. This lag in the speed of adoption is occasioned by the spontaneously imaginable life or death importance involved in the practical employment of critical and most effective tools, all of which must be static-load-tested et al. before risking human life, either as test pilot or as ultimate passenger aboard the aircraft.

Inventions in the automobile arts are adopted by their industry within an average span of ten years, and railroad inventions take eighteen years to become standardly employed.

While buildings expand and contract physically between summer's heat and winter's cold, and even between night and day temperatures, those size changings are invisible to the human eye. While buildings are stressed importantly by great wind loads and snow loads—great skyscrapers sway as much as a foot, but relatively slowly—the deflective motions are invisible to man. Invisible also are the motions of the hands of the clock, or of atomic components of matter, though the latter hither-and-yon radiationally and locally, as matter, at 700,000,000 m.p.h. speeds. So also invisible to man are the vast high-speed motions of the stars and the relatively slow growth of trees. When man cannot see the motion, he rarely thinks realistically about it. He is not prone to be usefully critical of the invisible, yet real, kinetics of design function suitability, nor of relative performance efficiency. Nor are humans inclined to put their experience to inventive advantage for others until they have had a long series of personal inconveniences and accidents to prompt them into comprehending the involved critical events which they cannot see. Humans tend to identify as machines only those complex devices which they can see move. Unable to see their buildings' seasonally slow energy transformations functioning as machines, which indeed they are, humans fail to design their buildings with the same degree of scientific integrity with which, for instance, they conduct the ten million discrete but mostly invisible tasks that have to be completed from the outset of "countdown" to the successful "blast-off" of a rocketed, humanly manned, extraterrestrially traveling capsule. As a consequence of humanity's inability to see the energy transformation motions involved, the structural design of its land buildings and its livingry mechanics, such as plumbing equipment, lag three thousand years behind the evolution in airspace technology standards. Humanity's housing structures and livingry in general are, to a high degree, only superstitiously evolved, economic prowess symbols, inefficiently repetitious of all of yesterday's make-do mistakes.

We can say that in respect to the directly recognized motion experiences of the average observer that the higher the operating velocity of the art involved, the shorter is the invention-to-industrialization lag. Electromagnetic communication, operating at 700 million miles per hour, has the least lag. Astronautics operating at between 10 and 20 thousand m.p.h., jetonautics at 200 to 1800 m.p.h., and automobiles at 0 to 150 m.p.h. follow one another in the rate of contraction of the relative magnitude of delayed invention adoption. They also rank in the same order in degree of nicety of design production and control. One quadrillionth of an inch in electromagnetic communications tuning capability, one ten millionth of an inch in astronautic mechanisms, one hundred thousandth of an inch in jetonautics, one ten thousandth of an inch in automobiles, and one sixteenth of an inch in the housebuilding arts. Housing, which seems to move not at all, has the greatest invention-to-use lag. The lag between invention and commercial use in skyscrapers is about twenty-five years; in single family dwellings the invention-to-industrialization-use lag is about forty-five to fifty years.

Because of the widely differing lags occurring between invention and common use as disclosed by the different arts, the twentieth-century Leonardo's conceptioning of mass production industry—as being essential to the gratification of the living needs of all humanity—as yet has come into effective world-around use only in the omni-invisible electronic and semi-invisible aeronautical, and partially invisible marine, automobile, and railroad technologies. Industrial mass production, which long ago produced nails, screws, bricks, and small parts of buildings, is favorably effecting the production of many of the parts going into the skyscraper phase of the building arts, but none of the synergetic benefits of scientifically coordinated high-speed, lightweight moving-line production and general assemblage of final user products—as mass-produced, distributed, maintained, and removed—only under the omni-controlled, optimum environmental conditions—and thereafter the mass delivery of fully assembled, ready-to-use, rentable-anywhere, scientifically serviced, complex dwelling machine products has been realized, as yet anywhere. Such competence will never be realized by the utterly obsolete, "one-off" handcrafting, under uncontrolled field conditions, as practiced by an interplay of real estaters, banks, contractors, building lobbies, and government subsidy. All that is now dead. It will be replaced by the high-priority airspace technologies of the world being reoriented from a war- to a peace-aimed economy.

Mass production industry as conceived and instituted by the modern Leonardos will not affect its ultimate beneficiary, the common man and his home-life dwelling facilities, in important degrees, until the mid-1970s, when the 45-50-year evolutionary transition lag between the 1927 invention of the Dymaxion House, the equivalent in dwelling machine, service industry facility to the "Model T," has run its course and mass proliferation of scientifically conceived, produced, delivered, maintained, and removed dwellings for all of humanity everywhere around the world will be realized in equal service satisfaction to that provided today by the rent-anywhere, leave-anywhere automobile facilities.

In the 1970s we will see skyscrapers mass-assembled, horizontally in the air-space industry's controlled condition factories, vertically airlifted in their horizontal, low air drag attitude to a position over their installation sites and then rotated into a vertical attitude, lowered and made fast to their anchored-piling foundations.

The 1970s will see air deliveries all around the world of semi-autonomous dwelling machines belonging to the world-around, computerized, universal credit card managed rental service systems which will air-install, maintain, and air-remove the dwelling machines within hours. The power to operate semi-autonomous sanitation automation and the equipment involved will be mass-produced from the experience gained in the moon and outer space programs and equipment prototyping. The little black boxes that contain all the life-regenerating systems will dispense forever with the Earthians' wasteful piped-in water supply and sewer systems. The only slowly and meagerly decreasing, essential chemistries of such recirculating systems will be replenished intermittently in small containers. Energy as electrical power will be beam-transmitted and satellite-relayed to humans operating anywhere within the solar system. Energy as Sun power will be universally employed.

In the first nine periods of the total history of the economic patronage of the creative individuals' initiatives, the hand fashioning of the environmental rearrangements, advantaging both the afterlife and the living lives, occurred under the conditions of humanity's thinking of reality as consisting strictly of the phenomena that could be apprehended directly by humanity's senses of sight, touch, hearing, smelling, and

61

tasting. All invisible occurrences were considered to be either mystical, magical, or trickery. Then came man's discovery of electromagnetics, atomic physics, and chemistry, and with them was opened to human exploration, discovery, and rearrangement formulations within the vast ranges of the invisible, non-sensorially contactible reality. Thereby all of yesterday's mysteries were either logically explained or dismissed.

During the first seven historical periods man thought of all men as totally conscious of themselves and consciously responsible for their every waking hour's act. In Period Eight Freud and Mesmer, through hypnosis, shook humanity's complacent assumption of an exclusively *conscious reality*. Period Ten's invisible electromagnetics, chemistry, biochemistry, and mathematics ushered in by the initiatives of the mass production invention of twentieth-century Leonardos—including the Einsteins, Bells, Wrights, Edisons, and even earlier Hertzs, Maxwells, Faradays, Boyles, et al.—made it evident to those who thought cogently about it that reality is more than 99 percent invisible. The swelling ranks of those trained scientifically to cope with the 99 percent invisibility of reality rendered humanity's exclusively visible, news-pictured undertakings almost negligibly important.

There is a clearly discernible successional order in which the various prime categories of humanity's capabilities come to employ, and to be almost miraculously advantaged by, the invisible reality's exquisite reliabilities of technical formulation. The first to so prospect was mathematical thought itself. Next came the communications arts; next came the air-space transportations arts; next the ground transportation; and lastly will come the world-around dwelling and livingry arts.

The latter evolutionary scheduling of events is a fact that 99 percent of humanity has not as yet come to understand, but that fact underlies the students' mid-60s intuitive rejection of all superficially based traditions.

Whereas the aesthetics of the first nine periods were sensorially apprehendible the Leonardo type humans' preoccupations in Period Ten have been predicated on an *utterly invisible aesthetic*. The aesthetics of Period Ten will probably govern the Leonardo type initiations of all centuries to come and will be the most important ingredient of humanity's survival—if those of the human team now aboard planet Earth do indeed survive.

The great *aesthetic* which will inaugurate the twenty-first century will be the utterly invisible quality of intellectual *integrity;* the integrity of the individual in dealing with his scientific discoveries; the integrity of the individual in dealing with conceptual realization of the comprehensive interrelatedness of all events; the integrity of the individual in dealing with the only experimentally arrived at information regarding invisible phenomena; and finally the integrity of all those who formulate invisibly within their respective minds and invisibly with the only mathematically dimensionable, advanced production technologies, on behalf of their fellow men.

This aesthetic of integrity causes the new life now emerging aboard our spaceship Earth to abhor any hypocrisy. Children are spontaneously truthful. They simply announce that which they observe. Lying and warping of information is an acquired capability. Panicking fear employs lying, in the mistaken hope that it will be advantageous. Because it is a fiction it can be dispelled. Corruption by lying requires a mental self-deceit, a misconception—a visualization of imagined experience. The unimaginableness of the invisible reality precludes such manipulation.

In the cold warring all that one side can do to the others is

63

to jam, obscure, or destroy the information because its meaning content cannot be perverted. The intuitions of the young are overwhelmed by the awareness of the utter essentiality of comprehensively operative information *integrity* to their present and future lives. They are forsaking all vain symbolism of pseudo "distinction."

The young are as imbued with idealism, harmonics, romance, and awareness of the a priori mystery of "How come Universe?" as have been all generations before them. But their passion for integrity will ensure them against the disappointment and dismays of earlier generations all of which were betrayed by ignorance, fallacious credos, axioms, and passionately biased customs promulgated by ruthless muscle-wielded swords or more latterly by the most powerful, gun-imposed dictatorships which taught their followers to lie as an act of loyalty. Youth's idealism and love of harmonic synchronization can only be guaranteed gratifyingly by the integrity to which their intuitions bind them.

Seeking an understanding of the comprehensive aesthetic trending throughout our ten past-period history we have traveled from an at first but dimly inferred review to a now *overwhelmingly documented* history of humanity's initiatives and accomplishments aboard planet Earth. We found humanity at earliest recorded times philosophically assuming an eternal *NOW* Universe. In it death did not mean departure from life but only a transformation or transmigration of the individual. Thereafter we go through an illogical dichotomy of Universe into two Universes, into Life and Lives-hereafter, a temporal, character-trial life, plus two other eternal Universes: Heaven and Hell. That is, three Universes, one an Earth-Time Universe—that had its *horizontal* planes laterally extensible outwardly from its "civilization" or tribal center to the land of

64

dragons and thence to infinity. Its perpendicular, up-and-down lines ran diametrically toward *two* separate timeless eternities, the Heaven and Hell Universes.

Throughout the first nine periods of the Leonardo type, era-transforming initiations we rewitnessed the realization of a series of major Earthian edifices which consisted at first of Naga, or water-surrounded, square-based, solidly packed, multi-pinnacled, rock and stone models of the world as it evolved slowly into single-pinnacled or one central-mountained world with climbable steps. Such edifices of Southeast Asia, Mesopotamia (ziggurats), and Central America simply informed society that this was the structural scheme of the gods, of whom their king was at first only one of many, ergo, many, mini-mountain spires in the complex, but later became "it," requiring only a one-pinnacled structure.

In our first eight successive periods as led by the Leonardo types' prime, teleological designing initiatives, the edifices became progressively occupied in ever increasing geometrical magnitude, first with a small subterranean chamber beneath the half-octahedronal, square-based, pyramidal edifices erected for the Pharaoh's entry into the afterlife. Thereafter in the successive Leonardian type's design revolution periods the interior of such edifices' accommodations were progressively amplified to house the afterlives of ever greater numbers of nobles and their attendants; and then were amplified even more to accommodate all the middle-class afterlifers as boxlike chambers above Earth, as mausoleums.

Such depositories of human remains for an afterlife continuation are not to be confused with the temples which are extensions of the earliest theology. The columned temples of Egypt, Asia Minor, the Greek and later Roman worlds were gradually evolved from the earliest invisible cathedral, "beauty" spots, *fung shui,* where the breathtaking beauty and view from the highest, tree-line altitudes mountain shoulders evoked humanity's most expansive thoughts and thanksgiving or prayer for further favors. The often worshiped and decorated trees on those beauty spots gradually died and were replaced by the formally decorated columns of the temples. The Greek temples were usually placed on the shoulder lands halfway toward mountain peaks so that while affording magnificent views which engendered humans' most noble conceptioning, there were always the much higher mountain peaks above to remind man of the far greater viewpoint and power of their gods. The temples were for temporal life's thanksgiving and beseeching.

Finally the edifices designed by the Leonardo type teleological initiators of this latter series of thanks-and-ask stone-forest edifices became at first the private, tiny chapel for exclusive use of their living king within which he might pray for help in his coming battle. This king's chapel period was followed by the relatively small thirteenth-century crusader-patronized abbeys of England. Then came the vast interior of the great cathedrals to accommodate preparations for everybody's afterlife and prayers for some favors in this life. But the mountain-peak architectural tradition of the early wats persisted, in the form of increasingly impressive spires superimposed on the prime cavernous church or cathedral, or the "mountain" spire became entirely detached from the cavernous houses of worship and prayer. Thus sometimes these man-occupiable caverns (duomos) have their exclusively god-occupiable, higher mountain as a separate outside tower (campanile). By this total overall evolution the once solid stone piles finally were penetrated in even greater degree until they became the cathedrals (meaning Universal, i.e., for all people). The cathedrals are finally relatively thin-shelled, orderly designed piles of externally buttressed stone. Chambers for depositing the bodies furthering afterlife were at first, as with pyramids, placed below the cathedral flooring but as more and more people had to be accommodated after life, the graveyards outside the cathedral developed.

Returning again to consideration of the mass production functioning of Period Nine, we find that it expanded reality ninety-ninefold to include the whole range of the invisible events of Universe. These had been held previously by humans to be magical and superstitiously mystical. Now they had become the realities of everyday science.

In Period Ten we witness the progressive abandonment of the cathedral and churches by an ever accelerating succession of individually intuitive withdrawals from religious groups not because the individual has less awareness of a greater wisdom and integrity operative than is ascribable to any known capabilities of humans, but simply because their further participation in dogmatic formula and the unthinking rituals of such religious ceremony was ever less acceptable as being truthfully cogent of the total informative environment.

Period Ten, which has much more to accomplish, is destined to emancipate all humanity from physical drudgery and conversely to give every individual the freedom to reemploy his original unblemished childhood's faculty of thought and experimental curiosity drives in whatever way each finds to be most constructive.

Thus we find that all the superstitional symbolism of yesterday's houses of worship have become irrelevant and obsolete, though redolent with pathos, regarding both the innocent devotion and trust placed upon the words of the dogma harnessed and devotedly considerate "fathers." The great cathedrals, smaller ministries, churches, temples, pyramids, ziggurats, ghats, and wats thus become ever more informative only as archaeological disclosures of the great human epic. As such they become increasingly inspirational as integrity seeks to understand and to appreciate the great dedications of the past, and to offset the errors of yesterday with ever greater fulfillment of humanity's conscious, metaphysical functioning in the evolutionary events of macro-medi-micro Universe.

Thus we find humanity beginning to recognize that science has discovered that there are no experimentally demonstrable static things. There are no solids; no *at-rest* statics. There are only *weightless metaphysical* and *weighable physical* energy events both characterized by irreversible proclivities and unique interferences, frequencies of oscillating symmetries and maximum asymmetries, complementaries, etc. There are no experimentally demonstrable things. We have no use for *nouns;* and can use only *verbs.* Newton's instant, noun-thing Universe has been replaced with Einstein's scenario, verb-event, wave-frequency Universe. There is no experimentally demonstrated phenomenon *space,* only experimentally disclosed, discrete packages of energy, as discontinuous quanta events.

As we saw earlier, we have *events* and *no-events, moments* and *no-ments.* There is no zero *time.* Time is always a duration-magnitude event. We have only *becoming* and *became.* We have only *yesterday* and *already begun tomorrow.* We have no static single frame Universe. We have only an aggregate of non-simultaneous and only partially overlapping experiences, subjective and objective—a scenario of separate quantum frames of electromagnetic reality events overridden by a plurality of omni-interaccommodative generalized behavioral laws which are utterly abstract, weightless, invisible, metaphysical concepts—manifesting an all-embracing integrity of intellection. We also have the disassociation of that weightless integrity which is unique to life from the physical regenerative chemical organism of seven pounds at birth, augmented twentyfold more at maturity.

This new era, Period Ten's cosmology, is ushered in by Einstein's "Cosmic Religious Sense," first published in the New York *Times* Sunday Magazine at New Year's of 1930, right after the great financial "crash" of 1929 in which latter the living gods of exclusively physical power were banished forever from the highest throne of human esteem. In the same year 1929 the ninety-second isolation of the total, finite family of ninety-two regenerative chemical elements was accomplished and the invisible-ingredients cupboard, of the invisible reality, was completely stocked to service the constructive assemblage of the invisible tenth period of history.

In the closing days of the twentieth century humanity seems to be returning into the Garden of Eden of an invisible, "edificeless," comprehensive integrity of an eternally self-transforming and regenerative Universe. In this tenth period all humanity will find itself intellectually empowered to teach itself through individual thought.

The god function in all humanity of the capability to think and act with teleologic-integrity will ever approach but never quite attain the perfection of absolute integrity which we now identify in utter abstraction as truth or god. God as a verb, as an abstract love-momentumed gyro-compass, will intuit the emergent directional courses to be steered. Otherwise, there will be no more humans aboard spaceship Earth and the metaphysical functions of orderly discernment and mastery of the physically disorderly behaviors of Universe will have to be carried on by minds operating elsewhere and otherwise in Universe.

For there are to be *Periods Eleven and Twelve* of Leonardo

type initiations of the design revolution to be realized by humanity somewhere in Universe to complementarily comprehend, cohere, and resonantly regenerate the discontinuous, positive-negative quantized universal evolution.

## Period Eleven

In Period *Eleven* the Leonardo types' economic-patronage mandate will be that of the newborn children of all humanity everywhere. In Period Eleven this Leonardo type will be preoccupied with the safeguarding of the innate faculties of the newborn. In historical Period Eleven it will be the function of the Leonardo type design revolutionary to compound for humanity the ever increasingly augmentable advantages inherent in the fact that each child is born in the presence of less cosmological and cosmogonal misinformation and is endowed with as yet undamaged, unfrustrated love drives to apprehend, comprehend to understand and be understood; to employ regeneratively the ever more reliable information, electronically retrievable by each individual, for private individual consumption; and thereby potentially, to discover and designingly employ on behalf of all humanity an ever greater inventory of the generalized principles interaccommodatively governing universal-metaphysical and physical evolution.

## Period Twelve

In historical Period *Twelve* it will be the function of the Leonardo type initiators of the design revolution to employ the evolutionary environment modifications capabilities, com-

70

ing ever more importantly within the domain of human potential, under the inspiring *patronage mandate* of all *the as yet unborn generations of humanity, ever-to-be-in-Universe,* while always ensuring the evolutionary advantage of all those now living as inspiringly informed by all the experiences, positive and negative, of all previous generations of mind in man.

And when Period Twelve of history has reached maturity and mind-in-man-in-Universe has masteringly explored vast time-distance ranges of the presently operative scenario "Universe"—and approximately all of the physical phenomena, once only superstitiously considered by humanity, will be electrochemically comprehended by humanity in general—humanity will have learned that the human organic, anatomical complex, identified as the human corpus or body, is exclusively physical, and constitutes the most anticipatorily successful self-regenerating and replica-reproducing automated machine design known to exist within Universe, being lesser only in evolutionary self-regenerating complexity to scenario "Universe" itself, wherefore man will have learned that life is not the machine but is the utterly weightless, immortal individual intellectual integrity. And when that degree of universal integrity of understanding has been attained by mind-in-man consciousness, all the questions of Universe will have converged into one great and forever unanswerable question.

"How come Universe?"—and its complex inventory of omni-non-contradictorially, intertransforming, and only partially overlapping, interaccommodative, abstract, weightless, generalized principles. This is a question which seems guaranteed to be eternal by virtue of the forever irreversible directional progression toward an infinitely non-attainable, ergo *timeless truth.* We can only approach but never attain *com-*

*pletely inclusive, infinitely incisive truth* or *love,* or *under-standing.*

The integrity of the loving dream is the integrity of Universe and being humanly unattainable is inherently uncorruptible and infinitely regenerative.

# EARTHIANS'
# CRITICAL MOMENT

# EARTHIANS'
# CRITICAL MOMENT

Now 75 and born before the automobile, radio, airplane or
cinema, my memory spans humanity's transition from a myriad of vastly isolated, popularly illiterate communities and
tribes . . . with only vague awareness of one another . . .
now converted into the beginning of an omni-integrated, freely
intercirculating, omni-literate world society.

I have seen humanity transformed from a condition of less
than 1 per cent to 40 per cent of the now doubled world population which is enjoying economic success and living standards superior to any pre-twentieth-century monarchs. Simultaneously the life span of that successful 40 per cent has been
doubled. Though large, that 40 per cent is, as yet, a "minority" of all humanity.

We are now entered into Earthians' most critical moment,
that of imminent, technically feasible economic success for
all humanity. This, however, is frustrated by the large and
prosperous minority's fearful procrastination at the entrance
into the unknown, epochal changes, obviously essential to
realization of comprehensive human success and total planetary freedoms and enjoyment.

On the other hand, the mortally concerned "have-not" majority and vast millions of their well-to-do, youthful, world-

around sympathizers are revolutionarily organized or revolution prone. This condition is worsened by the combined expenditures for weaponry, warring and adjunct activities, of all the opposing forces of the world, which now averages an annual two-hundred billion dollars.

This not only wastes humanity's highest productivity, but turns its capabilities and resources toward extinction of humanity. It postpones public discovery of its potential of total human success and deters serious consideration of the means to realize that success.

During my lifetime the world's physical resource reserves per each world human have continually decreased. Therefore, the eighty-folding of the numbers of economically successful within two-thirds of a century can be accounted for only as the unexpected by-product of the doing-ever-more-with-ever-less resources per each realized function, occasioned by the design science revolution initiated exclusively in world-around weaponry developments and their supporting production techniques. Humanity is acquiring the right technology for all the wrong reasons—and only as driven by looming wars and the fear of being annihilated by the enemy. Humanity could acquire the technology for the purpose of total success and enduring peace of humanity. Under these conditions in the past humans said "we cannot afford it in peace times," but when the technology is acquired it not only pays for itself, but always constitutes inadvertent acquisition of greater wealth.

The known total of in-mine or recirculatable chemical elements of the world is now preoccupied in serving only the 40 per cent minority. At the present halfway stage of the design revolution our resources cannot support economic success, health and expanded longevity for the 60 per cent "have-nots" of all humanity. This is due to the low level of engineering efficiency and capability of presently acceptable standards of technological strategy, i.e., an over-all of only 4 per cent realized of the 100 per cent energy employed.

This efficiency can be improved threefold to an over-all 12 per cent under now proven technological alternatives.

Political revolution, per se, can only take from one to advantage another. Yet total success for humanity could eliminate war. Total success can be accomplished only by:

• Shunting the high priority airspace electronics industry from preoccupation with killingry to preoccupation with livingry.

• The direct application to livingry purposes of the now known, but as yet unemployed, design science stratagems for producing ever-more-physical-performance-with-ever-less resources per function accomplished, and at the same time developing all humanity's spontaneous awareness of its realizable success and the technological nature of its fulfillment.

Such a cooperative spirit and initiative on an ever swifter and broadening scale is essential to realization of the design science revolution, without which humanity at large will undoubtedly perish.

# REVOLUTION
# IN WOMBLAND

# REVOLUTION
# IN WOMBLAND

At all times nowadays, there are approximately 66 million human beings around Earth who are living comfortably inside their mothers' wombs. The country called Nigeria embraces one-fourth of the human beings of the great continent of Africa. There are 66 million Nigerians. We can say that the number of people living in Wombland is about the same as one-fourth the population of Africa. This 66 million Womblanders tops the total population of either West Germany's 58 million, the United Kingdom's 55 million, Italy's 52 million, France's 50 million, or Mexico's 47 million. Only nine of the world's so-called countries (China, India, Soviet Union, United States, Indonesia, Pakistan, Japan, and Brazil) have individual populations greater than our luxuriously-living, under-nine-months-old Womblanders.

Seemingly switching our subject, but only for a moment, we note that for the last two decades scientists probing with electrodes have learned a great deal about the human brain. The brain gives off measurable energy and discrete wave patterns disclosed by the oscillograph. Specific, repetitive dreams have been identified by these wave patterns. The neurological and physiological explorers do not find it extravagant to speculate that we may learn that what humanity has thus far spoken of mystifiedly as telepathy, science will have discovered, within decades, to be ultra-ultra high-frequency electromagnetic wave propagations.

All good science fiction develops realistically that which scientific data suggests to be imminent. It is good science fiction to suppose that a superb telepathetic communication system is interlinking all those young citizens of worldaround Wombland. We intercept one of the conversations: "How are things over there with you?" Answer: "My mother is planning to call me either Joe or Mary. She doesn't know that my call frequency is already 7567-00-3821." Other: "My mother had better apply to those characters Watson, Crick, and Wilkerson for my call numbers!" And another of their 66 million Womblanders comes in with, "I'm getting very apprehensive about having to 'go outside.' We have been hearing from some of the kids who just got out—they say we are going to be cut off from the main supply. We are going to have to shovel fuel and pour liquids into our systems. We are going to have to make our own blood. We are going to have to start pumping some kind of gas into our lungs to purify our own blood. We are going to have to make ourselves into giants fifteen times our present size. Worst of all, we are going to have to learn to lie about everything. It's going to be a lot of work, very dangerous, and very discouraging." Answer: "Why don't we strike? We are in excellent posture for a 'sit-down.'" Other: "Wow! What an idea. We will have the whole population of worldaround Wombland refuse to go out at graduation day. Our cosmic population will enter more and more human women's wombs, each refusing to graduate at nine months. More and more Earthian women will get more and more burdened. Worldaround consternation—agony. We will notify the outsiders that, until they stop lying to themselves and to each other and give up their stupid sovereignties and exclusive holier-than-thou ideologies, pollutions, and mayhem, we are going to refuse to come out. Only surgery fatal to both the mothers and ourselves could evacuate us."

Another: "Great! We had might as well do it. If we do come out we will be faced with the proliferation of Cold War's guerrillerized killing of babies for psycho-shock demoralization of worldaround innocent communities inadvertently involved in the abstruse ideological warfare waged by diametrically opposed, equally stubborn, would-be do-gooder, bureaucratic leaders and their partisans who control all of the world's means of production and killing, whose numbers (including all the politically preoccupied individuals around the Earth) represent less than one per cent of all humanity, to whose human minds and hearts the politicos and their guns give neither satisfaction nor hope. Like the women in *Lysistrata* who refused intercourse with their men until they stopped fighting, we Womblanders would win."

Until yesterday, what are now the 150 member nations of our planet's United Nations were tiny groups of humans who for two million years had been regenerating around our globe so remotely from one another that each colony, nation, or tribe was utterly unaware of one another's existence. Only through telepathy, as supposedly operative in the previous paragraphs, could those remote cells of precariously-surviving human beings have been aware of one another throughout those two million years. In the last few split seconds of overall history, there emerged a dozen millennia ago from the womb of tribal remoteness a few sailors and overland explorers who began to discover the presence of other humans scattered around the mysterious world. Finding the tribes to be each unaware of either the surprising resources or the vital

83

needs and desires of the others, they kept the whereabouts of these surprise demands and supplies secret and thus were able, through monopoly of commerce and middle-manning, to exploit to their own special advantage the vital needs, ignorance, and the wealth of life-support to be generated by expediting or slowing the physical resource interactions with humanity's available time to work the resources into higher advantage tools, environment controlling devices, and metabolically regenerative sustainers.

Throughout all the two million years up to the Twentieth Century, the total distance covered by an average man in an average lifetime disclosed to him less than one millionth of the surface of our spherical planet. So tiny was a human and so relatively large is our planet that it is not surprising that humans as yet cerebrate only in terms of a "wide, wide world— a four-cornered Earth," situated in the middle of an infinite plane, to which all the perpendiculars are parallel to one another and lead only in two directions—UP and DOWN— with sky UP there and earth DOWN here.

No matter how you may look upon the matter morally and ideologically, the assumption that humanity could or could not own a piece of land with all the earth vertically below it and all the air vertically above it is not only scientifically invalid—it is scientifically impossible. The scheme is geometrically possible only as an up-and-down make-believe flat world.

To understand the scientific impossibility of such a scheme, let us consider a cube inside of a sphere, with the cube's eight corners congruent with the surface of the sphere. Let the cube's twelve edges consist of steel structurals. A light is at the common center of the cube and sphere and casts a shadow of the twelve structural edges of the cube outwardly upon the surface of the translucent sphere. We will now see that the total spherical surface is divided symmetrically by great circle arcs into six equilateral four-edged areas. Though each of the four-sided symmetrical areas has 120-degree corners instead of 90-degree corners, each is called a spherical square. Altogether they constitute a spherical cube.

We will now suppose the spherical cube to be the planet Earth. We will suppose that war and treaties have resulted in the total Earth's being divided equally amongst six sovereign groups—each empowered by its laws to grant deeds to properties within their respective spherical square surfaces on the planet, regardless of whether covered by water or not. We will suppose that, as at present, each of the world's major sovereign nations assumes the authority to deed or lease the titles to subdivisions of each of their respective lands to corporations, subgovernments, and individuals. All the legally recognized deeds to property anywhere around our Earth date back only to sovereign claims established and maintained exclusively by military might.

Now that we have the model of a cubical subdivision of the sphere, let us color our cube's six faces, respectively, red, orange, yellow, green, blue, and violet. Let Russia sovereignly possess the red face of the cube. Consider all the perpendiculars to the red face of the internally positioned cube as being the up and down perpendiculars defining the property claims to all the land *below* the surface and all the air *above* the surface. Under these conditions, it will be seen that the red square owns all the interior of the cube which occurs perpendicularly below that red surface square. Therefore, each of the six countries would be claiming exclusive possession of the same "whole" cube, which obviously invalidates each and all of their claims to only one-sixth of the cube. This realization is mildly reminiscent of Portia's admonition to Shylock that he must be able to cut loose his pound of flesh without letting a drop of blood.

"Alright," you say, "I will concede it is impossible to demonstrate the validity of the claims to the lands lying perpendicularly below my surface map without invalidating all other land owners of the world. Therefore, I will try to live on the surface of my land and just claim it and the airspace vertically above me." "Alright," we say to you, "what air are you talking about, because it just blew away." You retort testily, "I don't mean that nonsense . . . just the air geometrically above me. That is what I refer to when I say you are violating my airspace—you are violating my overhead geometry." "Alright," we say to you, "which stars were you looking at when you said, '. . . that space above me'? Our Earth has been revolved away from those stars. Other stars are now above us. Not only are we revolving, but we are simultaneously orbiting around the sun, while all the planets and stars are always in swift motion, but are so far away from us and our lives so short that we are unable to perceive those motions. The distances involved are so great that the light from the next star to the sun takes four and one-half years to come to our solar system while traveling 700 million miles per hour and the distance across our galaxy is more than 300,000 light years, while the next nearest of the millions of galaxies are multi-millions of light years away from our galactic nebula. With those kinds of distances in the heavens, the amount of star motion that you and I can detect in our lifetime is humanly unrecognizable. Most of the star speeds within their galaxies are in the order of only 100,000 miles per hour, which is a negligible speed beside light's speed of 700 million miles per hour."

Because all the stars in the Universe are in motion, our planet orbits rotatingly in an ever-changing, omni-circus of celestial events. There is no static geometry of omni-interrelationship of Universe events. Some of the stars you are looking at have not been there for a million years—some no longer exist. As Einstein and Planck discovered, "Universe is a scenario of non-simultaneous and only partially overlapping, transformative events." One frame in the scenario of caterpillar does not foretell the later scenario event of its transformation into butterfly. One frame of butterfly cannot tell you that the butterfly flies; only large time-sequence segments of the scenario can provide meaningful information. Cogitating on the myriads of stars apparently scattered in disorderly spherical array about the heavens, individuals often remark, as may you, "I wonder what is outside outside?"—asking for a one-frame answer, which is as unintelligent as asking, "Which word is the dictionary?" You know the order of the dictionary to be alphabetical, but its words do not read sequentially. Just hearing them read aloud, they make an only apparent, disorderly array. This is typical of the manner in which nature hides her orderliness in only apparent disorder.

Back to little space vehicle Earth and that question of property. The most that the individual could be entitled to own would be the inside of an infinitely thin blueprint of his land, because there is no geometry of space outside it and no exclusively occupiable land below. Our planet Earth is the home of all humans, but scientifically speaking it belongs only to Universe. It belongs equally to all humans. This is the natural, geometrical law. Any laws of man which contradict nature are unenforceable and specious.

Without the infinitely-extended lateral plane, the words up and down are meaningless. The airman initiated the correct descriptive terms "coming IN for a landing and going OUT." It is meaningful to say "INSTAIRS and OUTSTAIRS." Say it for a week and your senses will discover and notify that you are living on a planet.

What do you mean, "astronaut?" *We are all astronauts.* Always have been—but really! Never mind your "Never-mind-that-space-stuff, let's-be-practical, let's-get-down-to-Earth" talk—brain-talk as undisturbed by knowledge as is a parrot's brain-talk by any awareness born of thought. Brain is physical—weighable; thought is metaphysical—weightless. Many creatures have brains. Man alone has mind. Parrots cannot do algebra; only mind can abstract. Brains are physical devices for storing and retrieving special case experience data. Mind alone can discover and employ the generalized scientific principles found holding true in every special case experience.

Universe has disclosed to astrophysics an elegantly orderly inventory of ninety-two regenerative chemical elements, each with its unique behaviors, all of which are essential to the success of Universe. All are in continual interexchange within the total evolutionary process of Universe. Ignorant humans aboard space vehicle Earth are now screaming, "Pollution!" There is no such phenomenon. What they call pollution is extraordinarily valuable chemistry essential to Universe and essential to man on Earth. What is happening is that the egocentricity of omni-specialized man makes him ignorant of the value with which his processing is confronting him. The yellow-brown content of fume and smog is mostly sulphur. The amount of sulphur going out of the smokestacks around the world each year is exactly the same as the amount of sulphur being taken from the Earth each year to keep the world ecology going. It would be far less expensive to catch that sulphur while concentrated in the stack, and to distribute it to the original users, than to do the original mining AND to get it out of human lungs, et cetera, when all the costs to society

88

over a deteriorating twenty-five years are taken into account. But humanity insists on holding to this year's profits, crops, and elections. World society is lethally shortsighted.

Subconsciously reflexing to the as yet mistaken concept of an infinite plane, men have felt that they could dispose of annoyingly accruing substances with which they did not know how to deal by dispatching them outward in some cosmic direction, assumedly to be diffused innocuously in infinity. "I spit in the ocean. So what?" Humans as yet cerebrate secretly and hopefully that—inasmuch as yesterday's exhaustion of customary resources has always been followed by discovery of alternate and better resources—the great infinity is going to keep right on taking care of ignorant carelessness and waste. "So what the hell?" say the "down-to-earth" status-quoers. "Pump all the fossil fuel energy-depositing of billions of years out from the Earth's crust. Burn it up in a century. Fill all your bank accounts with ten-place figures. To hell with the great grandchildren. Let them burn up our space vehicle Earth's oceans with hydrogen fusion. Let them do the worrying about tomorrow."

Just as biological protoplasmic cells are colonized into larger organisms, the most complex and omni-adaptable of which is the human, so too do humans colonize and inventively externalize the same organic tool functions for their mutual metabolic regeneration. We call this complex mutual tool externalization by the name industrialization, in which each of us can use the telephone or the electric light in our special, unique tasks, all of which require increasing development of world-around access to the total resources and world-around distribution of the advantages comprehensively produced in total metabolic regeneration.

The world population which, after the cell-colonizing

within its controlled environment, has been emitted from the thin, protoplasmic, tissue-sheathed, human womb into planet Earth's larger biosphere-sheathed, industrial organism womb, goes on colonizing, integrating, and specializing locally as innocently and ignorantly as did the protoplasmic cells within the woman's womb, all the while mistrusting one another as they evolve their utter interdependence around Earth, as do the individual protoplasmic cells of the residents of human Wombland gather together selectively, finally to form a whole child. In due course, we will realize a one world human integrity and with each degree of physical integration a new degree of metaphysical freedom will be attained.

Earthians in their more roomy biosphere are as yet provided for, despite their utter ignorance of the infinitely-exquisite reliable interactions of cosmic mechanics. Mothers don't have to invent a breast to feed the baby or invent oxygen for it to breathe. Nor do they have to tell the child how to invent its cell growth. Humans are utterly ignorant of what goes on, how, and why.

The Universe is a self-regenerating and transforming organic machine. Human womb graduates now gestating within the biosphere's world industrial organism womb are discovering and employing a few of the principles governing micro-macro cosmic mechanics, all the while ignorantly speaking of their accomplishments of the generally-disregarded obvious as "inventions" and "creations." Now humans have become suspicious of their little machines, blaming them for the continual disconnects of the inexorable evolutionary processes of cosmic gestations which—transcendental to their brain detecting—ever and again emit them into a greater, more inclusively exquisite spherical environment of automated mechanical controls that progressively decontrol humanity's thought and action capabilities—ever increasing humanity's options

90

—emancipating it from its former almost total preoccupation with absolute survival factors.

Assuming erroneously that their day-to-day positive experiences should be rendered perpetual and their negative experiences eliminated, humans try to freeze the unfreezable evolution at specific stages. They try to make "plastic flowers" of all momentarily satisfying events and paraphernalia. In the past, they tried to do it with stone. Separated from the familiar, confronted with the unfamiliar, and reflexed only by the brain's mechanical feedback, unthinking humans—not realizing that there are no straight lines, only wavy ones, and not realizing that waves can only be propagated by positive-negative oscillating—find their straight linear strivings forever frustrated by the wave system realities of Universe. Ignorantly they speak of the evolutionary waves' regeneratively oscillating complementaries as "good" and "bad," though the scientist can find no such moral and immoral qualities in the electron or its complementary opposite, the positron.

Humanity as a whole is indeed being emitted from a two-million-year gestation within the womb of permitted ignorance, for which infantile period cosmic mechanics have been making ample provision not only to offset ignorance and waste but also to permit humanity's gradual trial-and-error experimental discovery of the relatively negligible effectiveness of its muscle—which it had at first employed not only exclusively but savagely—and the concomitant discovery of the infinite apprehending and comprehending effectiveness of the human mind, which alone can discover and employ the Universal verities—and thereby realize comprehensively the potential, progressive, non-wasteful, competent, considerate mastery of the physical environment by the metaphysical intellect.

The metaphysical integrities manifest throughout the everywhere intertransforming Universe's omni-interaccommodative cosmic organic system apparently are from time-to-time emulated in meager degree by the intellect of the human passengers who are gestating within the spherical womb sheath of planet Earth's watery, gaseous, and electromagnetic biosphere.

Humanity's most recent sorties to the moon from within space vehicle Earth's womb-like biosphere sheath have been tantamount to a premature, temporary surgical removal of a baby from its human mother's womb, skillfully enclosed within a scientifically-controlled environment, still attached to the mother, and after successful surgery being returned into the human mother's womb to loll-out its remaining gestation days to the successful detached-action launching outwards in Universe which we ignorantly identify as "birth." Sovereign nation "landing cards" require answers to ridiculous questions: "When were you born?" "Where do you live?" Answer: "I am immortal. I check in here and there from celestial-time-to-celestial-time. Right now I am a passenger on space vehicle Earth zooming about the Sun at 60,-000 miles per hour somewhere in the solar system, which is God-only-knows where in the scenario Universe. Why do you ask?"

Humanity's sorties to the moon have been accomplished only through instrumental guidance of their controlled-environment capsules and mechanical-enclosure clothing by utterly invisible electromagnetic wave phenomena referenced to instrument-aligned star bearings, with the invisible mathematical integrations accomplished by computers, uncorrupted and incorruptible by ignorantly opinionated humans. Thus has man been advantaged by the few who have thought and acted to produce the instruments, as yet relieving the vast majority of humans from the necessity of having to think and co-ordinate their sensings with the realities of cosmic mechanics.

Humans still think in terms of an entirely superficial game of static things—solids, surfaces, or straight lines—despite that no things—no continuums—only discontinuous, energy quanta—separate event packages—operate as remotely from one another as the stars of the Milky Way. Science has found no "things"; only events. Universe has no nouns; only verbs. Don't say self-comfortingly to yourself or to me that you have found the old way of getting along with false notions to be quite adequate and satisfactory. So was the old umbilical cord to your mother. But you can't re-attach it and your mother is no longer physically present. You can't go back. You can't stay put. You can only grow and, if you comprehend what is going on, you will find it ever more satisfactory and fascinating, for that is what evolution is doing, whether you think, ignorantly, that you don't like it or do.

To each human being, environment is "all of Universe that isn't me." Our macrocosmic and microcosmic "isn't me-ness" consists entirely of widely dissynchronous frequencies of repetitions of angular changes and complex interactions of waves of different lengths and frequencies of repetition. Physics has found a Universe consisting only of frequency and angle modulations.

Our environment is a complex of frequencies and angles. Our environment is a complex of different frequencies of impingement—from within and without—upon the individual "me-nesses." We are in a womb of complex frequencies. Some of those frequencies man identifies ignorantly with such words as "sight, sound, touch, and smell." Others he calls "tornadoes, earthquakes, novae." Some he ignorantly looks

93

upon as static *things:* houses, rocks, and human-like manikins.

Very, very slow changes humans identify as inanimate. Slow change of pattern they call animate and natural. Fast changes they call explosive, and faster events than that humans cannot sense directly. They can see the rocket blasted off at 7,000 miles per hour. They cannot see the hundred-thousand times faster radar pulse moving 700 million miles per hour. Humans can sense only the position of pointers on instrument dials. What they call "radio"—electromagnetics—they learn of through scientific instrumentation. Of the total electro-mechanical spectrum range of the now known realities of Universe, man has the sensory equipment to tune in directly with but one millionth of the thus far discovered physical Universe events. Awareness of all the rest of the millionfold greater-than-human-sense reality can only be relayed to human ken through instruments, devised by a handful of thought-employing individuals anticipating thoughtfully the looming needs of others.

The almost totally invisible, nonsensorial, electromagnetic wombsheath of environmental evolution's reality-phase into which humanity is now being born—after two million years of ignorant, innocent gestation—is as yet almost entirely uncomprehended by humanity. Ninety-nine and nine tenths per cent of all that is now transpiring in human activity and interaction with nature is taking place within the realms of reality which are utterly invisible, inaudible, unsmellable, untouchable by human senses. But the invisible reality has its own behavioral rules which are entirely transcendental to man-made laws and evaluation limitations. The invisible reality's integrities are infinitely reliable. It can only be comprehended by metaphysical mind, guided by bearings toward something sensed as truth. Only metaphysical mind can communicate.

Brain is only an information storing and retrieving instrument. Telephones cannot communicate; only the humans who use the instruments. Man is metaphysical mind. No mind—no communication—no man. Physical transactions without mind —YES. Communication—NO. Man is a self-contained, micro-communicating system. Humanity is a macro-communicating system. Universe is a serial communicating system; a scenario of only partially overlapping, nonsimultaneous, irreversible, transformative events.

As yet preoccupied only with visible, static, newspicture views of superficial surfaces of people and things—with a one-millionth fraction of reality which it has cartooned in utter falsehood—society fails to realize that several hundred thousand radio or TV communications are at all times invisibly present everywhere around our planet. They permeate every room in every building—passing right through walls and human tissue. This is to say that the stone walls and human tissue are invisible and nonexistent to the electromagnetic wave reality. We only deceived ourselves into reflexing that the walls are solid. How do you see through your solid eyeglasses? They are not full of holes. They are aggregates of atoms as remote from one another as are the stars. There's plenty of space for the waves of light to penetrate.

Several hundred thousand different wide-band radio sets can at any time be tuned in anywhere around our biosphere to as many different communications. Going right through our heads now, these programs could be tuned in by the right crystals and circuits. Crystals and circuits consist of logically structured atomic arrays. Such arrays could operate even within our brains. Tiny bats fly in the dark by locating objects ahead in their flight path by ever more minuscule radar sending and receiving, distance-to-object calculating mechanisms. Right this minute, five hundred Earth-launched satellites with sensors are reporting all phenomena situated about our planet's surface. Tune in the right wavelength and learn where every beef cattle or every cloud is located around the Earth. All that information *is* now being broadcast continually and invisibly.

For humans to have within their cerebral mechanism the proper atomic radio transceivers to carry on telepathetic communication is no more incredible than the transistors which were invented only two decades ago, and far less incredible than the containment of the bat's radar and range-finding computer within its pin-point size brain. There is nothing in the scientific data which says the following thoughts are impossible and there is much in the data which suggests that they are probable. The thoughts go as follows: The light of a candle broadcasting its radiation in all directions can be seen no farther than a mile away in clear atmosphere. When the same candle's flame is placed close in to the focus of a parabolic reflector and its rays are even further concentrated into a beam by a Freznell lens, its light can be seen at ten miles distance. The earliest lighthouses were furnished with such reflectively concentrated beam lights of tiny oil lamps.

What we speak of as light is a limited set of frequencies of the vast electromagnetic wave ranges. All electromagnetic waves can be beamed as well as broadcast. When beamed and lensingly concentrated (as with the laser beams refracted through rubies), their energies are so concentrated as to be able to bore tunnels in mountains. The shorter the waves, the smaller the reflector and refractor may be.

We know that the human has never seen outside himself. Electromagnetic waves of light bounce off objects outside him and frequencies are picked up by the human eyes and scanningly relayed back into the brain. Because the light

96

is so much faster than touch, smell, and hearing, men have tended to discount the billionth of a second it takes light to bounce off one's hand and to get the information back into one's brain. All sensing is done by humans entirely inside the brain, with information nerve-relayed from the external contact receivers. The human brain is like a major television studio-station. Not only does the brain monitor all the incoming live, visible, audible, smellable, and touchable 3D shows, it also makes videotapes of the incoming news, continually recalls yesterday's relevant documentaries and compares them with incoming news to differentiate out the discovered new and unexpected events from the long-familiar types, and to discover the implications of the news from those previously-experienced similar events, in order swiftly to design new scenarios of further actions logically to be taken in respect to the newly-evolved challenges.

So faithful has been the 4D, omni-directional, image-ination within the human omni-sense transceiving studio-stations of human brains that the humans themselves long ago came to assume spontaneously that the information received inside the brain made it safe to presume that those events were, in fact, taking place outside and remote from the seeing human individual. The reliability of all this imagining has been so constant that he now tends to think he sees only outside himself.

The shorter the electromagnetic, air, water, sand, or rocky earthquake wavelengths, the higher their frequency. The higher the wave frequencies, the more the possibility of their interfering with other high-frequency, physical phenomena such as walls, trees, mountains. The nearer they approach the same frequencies, the less do they interfere with one another. For this reason, the very high-frequency electromagnetic waves of radio and television get badly deflected by obstacles.

As a consequence, man learned to beam short wave television programs from horizon to horizon. He developed parabolic transceiver reflectioning cups that took in and sent out waves in parallel beam-focused rays. At the transceiver relay stations on the horizons, additional energy is fed into the signals received and their projection power is boosted so that, when they arrive at final destination after many relayings, their fidelity and power are as yet exquisitely differentiated and clearly resonated.

It may well be that human eyes are just such infra-sized parabolic transceiver cups. It may be that our transceiver eyes adequately accommodate the extraordinarily low magnitude of energy propagating of the brain as electromagnetic wave pattern oscillations to be picked up by others.

Early photography required whole minutes of exposure. As film chemistry improved, exposure times decreased. Yesterday, one thousandth of a second was fast. Today's capability makes one millionth of a second a relatively slow electro-astrophotography exposure. Pictures taken in a millionth of a second today are clearer than those of yesterday which took minutes. The scanned-out picture signals travel 700 million miles per hour. The effect in terms of man's tactile, hearing, and smelling senses is instantaneous.

Speakers who appear frequently before large audiences of human beings over a period of years have learned that the eyes of the audience "talk back" so instantaneously to them that they know just what their audiences are thinking and they can converse with their audiences, even though the speaker seems to be the only one making audible words. The feedback by eye is so swift as to give him instantaneous, spontaneous reaction and appropriate thought formulation.

The parabolic reflector-beamed, ultra-ultra high frequency, electromagnetic waves—such as can be coped with by transceivers with the infra-diameter of the human eye—are such that they would be completely interfered with by walls or other to-us-seemingly-opaque objects. However, when they are beamed outwardly to the sky in a cloudless atmosphere, no interference occurs. Ultra short wave radio and radar beams which are interfered with by mountains and trees can be beamed into a clear sky and bounced off the moon, to be received back on Earth in approximately one and three-fourths seconds. In a like manner, it is possible that human eyes operating as transceivers, all unbeknownst to us, may be beaming our thoughts out into the great night-sky void, not even having the sun's radiation to interfere mildly with them. Such eye-beamed thoughts sent off through the intercelestial voids might bounce off various objects at varying time periods, being reflectively re-angled to a new direction in Universe without important energy loss. A sufficient number of bouncings-off of a sufficient number of asteroids and cosmic dust could convert the beams into wide-angle sprays which diffuse their energy signals in so many angular directions as to reduce them below receptor-detection level. Eye-beamed thoughts might bounce off objects so remote as to delay their 700 million mile per hour travel back to Earth for a thousand years, ten thousand years, a hundred thousand years. It is quite possible that thoughts may be eye-beamed outwardly not only from Earth to bounce back to Earth at some later period from some celestially-mirroring object, but also that thoughts might be beamed—through non-interfering space to be accidentally received upon Earth—from other planets elsewhere in Universe. There is nothing in the data to suggest that the phenomenon we speak of as *intuitive thought* may not be just such remote cosmic transmissions. Intuitions come to us often with surprising lucidity and abruptness. Such intuitions often spotlight significant coincidences in a myriad of special case experiences which lead to discovery of generalized scientific principles heretofore eluding humanity's thought. These intuitions could be messages to the Earthian brain receiving it to "Look into so-and-so and so-and-so and you will find something significant." Intuitions could be thoughts dispatched from unbelievably long ago and from unbelievably far away.

As Holton wrote in the *American Journal of Physics* and as reported on the "Science" page of *Time* magazine, January 26, 1970:

> To fully recognize the extraordinary intellectual daring of Einstein's equations, we note the great scientist's own explanation of their origin: "There is no logical way to the discovery of these elementary laws. There is only the way of intuition."

Because humans consist of a myriad of atoms and because atoms are themselves electromagnetic frequency event phenomena—not things—it is theoretically possible that the complex frequencies of which humans are constituted, together with their angular interpositioning, could be scanningly unraveled and transmitted beamwise into the celestial void to be received some time, somewhere in Universe, having traveled at 700 million miles per hour, which is approximately 100 thousand times faster than the speed of our moon rockets a minute after blast-off. It is not theoretically impossible in terms of the total physical data that humans may have been transmitted to Earth in the past from vast distances.

Retreating from such a speculative mood, we come now to consider closer-range possibilities and probabilities. We recall that humans, who to our knowledge arrived on Earth at least two million years ago, have been regenerating aboard that small, 8,000-mile diameter, space vehicle Earth throughout all those years without even knowing that they were aboard a space vehicle. They are now emerging, however, from the womb of permitted ignorance of their early, subjective, taken-care-of phase and are now beginning to become comprehensively aware of all the matters we have discussed so far. They are beginning to understand that they are within a limited biosphere life-support system whose original excessively-abundant living supply was provided only to permit humanity's initial trial-and-error discovery of its antientropic function in Universe. Humans are coming swiftly to understand they must now consciously begin to operate their space vehicle Earth with total planetary cooperation, competence, and integrity. Humans are swiftly sensing that the cushioning tolerance for their initial error has become approximately exhausted.

Each child emerging from its mother's womb is entering a larger womb of total human consciousness which is continually modified and expanded by subjective experiences and objective experiments. As each successive child is born, it comes into a cosmic consciousness in which it is confronted with less misinformation than yesterday and with more reliable information than yesterday. Each child is born into a much larger womb of more intellectually competent consciousness.

I was seven years old before I saw an automobile, though living in the ambience of a large American city. Not until I was nine was the airplane invented. As a child I thought spontaneously only in terms of walking, bicycling, horse-drawn capability. Trips on railroads and steamships were dream-provokers learned of through a few older people who traveled. My daughter was born with cloth-covered-wing bi-planes in her sky and the talkie radio in her hearing. My granddaughter was born in a house with several jet transports going over every minute. She saw a thousand airplanes before she saw a bird: a thousand automobiles before a horse. To children

101

born in 1970, trips to the moon will be as everyday an event as were trips into the big city to me when a boy. There was no radio when I was born. Television came when I was what is called "retiring age." The first Berkeley dissident students were born the year commercial television started. They have seen around the world on the hour ever since being born— they think world. The total distance covered by an average human being in a total lifetime up to the time I was born was 30,000 miles. Because of the great changes since my birth, I have now gone well over one hundred times that distance. The astronauts knock off three million miles in a week. The average airline hostess is out-mileaging my hundredfold greater mileage than all the people before me. All this has happened in my lifetime. My lifetime has been one of emerging from the womb of human-being remoteness from one another to comprehensive integration of worldaround humanity. But all the customs, all the languages, all laws, all accounting systems, viewpoints, clichés, and axioms are of the old, divided, ignorant days. The corollary of "divide and conquer" is "to be divided is to be conquered." To be specialized is to be divided. The specialization which humanity perseveres in was invented by yesterday's armed conqueror illiterates. The separation of humans into more countries made them easy to manage. Nations may unite, as at present, without success. Strife is proliferating. Not until specialization and nations are dispensed with will humanity have a chance of survival. It is to be all or none.

In my first jobs before World War I, I found all the working men to have vocabularies of no more than one hundred words, more than 50 per cent of which were profane or obscene. Because I worked with them, I know that their intellects were there, but dulled and deprived of the information of visionary conceptioning. They had no way of expressing

102

themselves other than by inflection and shock. Conquerors invented gladiatorial wrestling, self-brutalizing games, slapstick and illusionary drama to keep their illiterate masses preoccupied when not at work. This was not changed by any scheduled system of education—it was changed by the radio. The radio broadcasting employees were hired for their vocabularies and diction. The eyes and ears of human beings were able to coordinate the words of the radio and the graphic words of the newspaper. Literacy accelerated. In a half-century, world-around man's vocabulary has been expanded to the equivalent of yesterday's scholar. Television's scientific invention and underwater and space exploration have accelerated this process of freeing humanity from its slave complex to an extraordinary degree. The young realize, as their elders do not, that humanity can do and can afford to do anything it needs to do that it knows how to do.

Those who ignorantly think of themselves as a well-to-do conservative elite are, in fact, so slave-complexed that they are shocked when the younger generation throws aside their clothes and cars of distinction and—abandoning their make-believe mansions which only are their old conquerors' castles —congregate in hundreds of thousands in shameless, innocent bands on vast beaches and meadows. It is not an unspannable generation gap that has occurred, but an emancipation of youth from yesterday's slave-complex reflexes. This has been brought about solely by the proliferation of knowledge. "The medium is the message" is the message only of yesterday's middle-class elite. It said, "Never mind the mind. It's the body that counts," or "It's the physical that can be possessed —To hell with the metaphysical. You can possess a physical brain but not the universally free mind and its thoughts. Leave that to the intellectuals. Look out for those dangerous free thinkers." Higher education was an adornment—a mark

103

of distinction—not something to be taken seriously. The problem of man's being born into the new womb of planetary comprehension, into the new world of integrated coordination and understanding of all humanity, is one not of educating a single absolute monarch, nor of educating either a fascistic or central party elite, nor of educating only the middle class. It is a matter of educating everyone everywhere to the realities of the emerging of man from the womb of permitted ignorance into the womb of required comprehension and competence. That education will have to be brought about by the extraordinary discarding of yesterday's inadequate amusements, shallow romances and drama, and make-believe substitute worlds to cover up the inadequacies of misinformed and underinformed, physically slavish or bureaucratically dogmatic, thoughtless life.

All the foregoing observations of human misorientations constitute but a minor fraction of those which can be truthfully and cogently made today with some chance of their not only being heard but heeded. And all this brings us all to this book by Gene Youngblood—an excellent name for one of the first of the youth who have emerged from childhood and schooling and "social experience" sufficiently undamaged to be able to cope lucidly with the problem of providing world-around man with the most effective communication techniques for speaking universal language to universal man— for helping universal man to understand the great transitions, to understand the reasonableness of yesterday's only-transitional inadequacies, to understand that the oldsters are victims of yesterday's ignorance and not Machiavellian enemies of youth, to understand that any bias—one way or another —utterly vitiates competent thinking and action, to understand that 100 per cent tolerance for error of viewpoint and

misbehavior of others is essential to new-era competence—
and, finally, to understand that man wants to understand. Nowhere have we encountered a youth more orderly-minded
regarding the most comprehensively favorable, forward functioning of humans in Scenario-Universe than in Gene Youngblood. His book *Expanded Cinema* is his own name for the
forward, omni-humanity educating function of man's total
communication system.

Isaac Newton, as the greatest Olympian of classical science
whose influence reigned supreme until the turn of the nine-
teenth into the twentieth century, assumed the Universe to be
*normally at rest* and abnormally in motion. Einstein realized
that the experimental data regarding the Brownian Move-
ment and the speed of light made it clear that Universe was
not normally at rest, for when its energies were released in a
vacuumized tunnel they traveled linearly at 186,000 miles per
second. This he assumed to manifest its norm, since that is
how Universe behaves normally when unfettered in a vacuum.
Any seemingly motionless phenomena, he reasoned, such as
seemingly solid matter, consisted of energy moving at 186,-
000 miles per second but in such small local orbits that their
speed and the exquisitely small, self-huddling orbit made
them impenetrable; ergo, apparently solid. This was the
basis of his formulation of his extraordinary $E=Mc^2$, which,
when fission and fusion occurred, proved his locked-up-
energy formulation to be correct. The utter difference between
Newton's norm of *at rest* and Einstein's norm of 186,-
000 miles per second provides humanity's most abrupt con-
frontation regarding the epochal difference of conceptioning
between that in the womb of yesterday's ignorance and in the
womb of new-dawning awareness, from which and into which,
respectively, man is now experiencing the last phases of delivery.

Thinking in terms of 700 million miles per hour as being normal—and informed by the experiments of scientists that no energies are lost—Einstein abandoned the Newtonian thought of Universe and assumed in its place Universe to be "A scenario of nonsimultaneous and only partially overlapping transformative events." Einstein's observational formulations, however, are subjective, not objective. In the mid-1930s I suggested in a book that Einstein's work would eventually affect the everyday environment of humanity, both physically and mentally. After reading what I had written, Einstein said to me, "Young man, you amaze me. I cannot conceive of anything I have ever done as having the slightest practical application." He said that to me a year before Hahn, Stressman, and Lisa Meitner had, on the basis of $E=Mc^2$, discovered the theoretical possibility of fission. You can imagine Einstein's dismay when Hiroshima became the first "practical application."

Gene Youngblood's book is the most brilliant conceptioning of the objectively *positive use* of the Scenario-Universe principle, which must be employed by humanity to synchronize its senses and its knowledge in time to ensure the continuance of that little, three-and-one-half-billion-member team of humanity now installed by evolution aboard our little space vehicle Earth. Gene Youngblood's book represents the most important metaphysical scenario for coping with all of the ills of educational systems based only on yesterday's Newtonian-type thinking. Youngblood's *Expanded Cinema* is the beginning of the new era educational system itself. Tomorrow's youth will employ the video cassette resources to bring in the scenario documents of all of humanity's most capable thinkers and conceivers. Only through the scenario can man possibly "house clean" swiftly enough the conceptual resources of his spontaneous formulations. Tomorrow's Ex-

106

panded Cinema University, as the word uni-verse—toward one—implies, will weld metaphysically together the world community of man by the flux of understanding and the spontaneously truthful integrity of the child.

# INEXORABLE EVOLUTION
# AND HUMAN ECOLOGY

## INEXORABLE EVOLUTION
## AND HUMAN ECOLOGY


Until humanity starts behaving
In logical ways
For logical reasons
Natural evolution will force it
To keep on behaving logically
For seemingly illogical reasons—
Resulting inexorably, as at present,
In humanity's backing
Rump-bumpingly into its future
While disregarding opportunities
To about-face and realize
Its inspiring passengership
Aboard Planet Earth—
As its exploratory mothership
Of ever vaster and more exquisite
Macro- and micro-cosmic realms.
And the frustrations
Of fearfully clung-to customs
Will persist unabated until
Humanity undertakes
Seriously, imaginatively,

Courageously, inspiringly
To employ effectively
The ever-more with ever less—
Of effort, material, time
And tolerance of error
Per each accomplished task
The comprehensively anticipatory
Design science revolution—
Being intent thereby
To make all of humanity
Successful in every sense.
As it undertakes design revolution
Humanity also must realize
That it can always afford rearrangements
Of the physical environment constituents
Which produce sustainable increases
In the proportion of all of humanity
Enjoying comprehensive success—
Provided only the task
Is physically feasible
Within ecologically critical limits
Of electro-magnetics, chemistry, time.
"We cannot afford" assumes spending
Intertransforming as matter or radiation
Energy cannot be spent
Know-how always increases
Wealth multiplies irreversibly.
And not until then will nature
Cease to cope with humanity's
Ignorance-prolonged inertia
Just in the same way
That human parents
Cope with their newborns'

Innocently ignorant
Self-helplessness—
And that is by forcing man
To acquire the adequate technology
With which ultimately
To attain and sustain
That potential omni-success.
And until then it will be accomplished inversely—
Through activating humanity's
Death fearing instincts.
Fear forcing it to acquire
The adequate production-tool complex
As a consequence of inducing humanity
Into an investment and reinvestment
Of its best capabilities and resources
Only in preparation for war.
This inverse procedure will regenerate
To ever higher degree
Both the more-with-less energy processing
And its production equipment.
And when man learns, if he does
To initiate the more-with-lessing
Under peacefully purposed auspices
Peace then will be attained
And Universe sustained
But not until then.

# VERTICAL IS TO LIVE—
# HORIZONTAL IS TO DIE

# VERTICAL IS TO LIVE—
# HORIZONTAL IS TO DIE

Memories of being cradle-songed circa 1896—Rock-a-Baby
. . . tree top . . . wind blow . . . cradle fall . . . down come
baby . . . cradle all—at which critical moment the baby was
zoomed at arms' length to above the grown-up's head and
thence swung almost to the floor for a thrill ride often to
shock-stop its crying. A popular 1920s song was titled "Baby
fa down and go boom." Babies live horizontally for months
before they spontaneously take the initiative and, coordinating
their own complex of control facilities, stand vertically. Vertical is objective. Horizontal is subjective, yielding. In extreme,
the vertical characterizes life and the horizontal characterizes
death.

From a continuous multiplicity of inadvertent bodily falling
and deliberately dropped objects, children learn from birth
onward that no one force operating in their lives is so constant,
unforgiving and relentless as gravity. Verticality opposes gravity. Behavioral science finds that fear is most powerfully incul-
cated in children by unexpectedly punishing falls. Horizontal
travel is easy and relatively safe. Vertical ascent by tree or
mountain climbing is arduous. Gravity clings at the climber.
Vertical descent yielding to gravity is hazardous and tends to
accelerate to an uncontrollable degree. Horizontal collisions

can be painful but, if visually anticipatable, are easily avoided —by putting on the muscular leg brakes. There are no brakes the child, falling vertically from a height, can use. Because their early walk-and-fall "sit-downs" shock their rumps and communicate important information to the children, their rumps are instinctively employed by the punitive type of parents for spank-shocking the child into learning additional lessons. The rumpshock admonishes the brain to signal the mind to discern what it may be that Universe is trying to induce the child to comprehend—not in words, but as a pure abstract, subconsciously recognized principle. Early experiments teach the child that he can't walk on water. Getting water in their noses when they put their heads under, plus their sinkability, arouses fear of deep water in many, but not all, children. Discovery of their ability to swim converts the fear into thoughtful respect for great waters. The data of experience make it scientifically demonstrable that the more dramatically conceptual and imaginatively feelable are both the threat of death, for self or others, and the experience-informed means for avoiding death or serious injury, the more integrity of thought and action humanity invests in its explorations, experiments, inventions and design science. Most powerful of all the subconscious factors unwittingly dominating humanity's teleological invention and design of vehicles of the land, sea and sky is its sense of relentless gravity.

Automobiles operate most frequently on horizontal surfaces or are oriented at approximately ninety degrees to gravity; when there is a "blowout" the vehicle can fall to the roadway no farther than the few inches of its maximum pneumatic tire elevation. Having little preconditioning experience with bad brakes, man operates horizontally without apprehension even though he always drives his autos within the linear "tubes" formed by the highway, roadside trees, bushes and buildings.

Within these "tubes" his automobiles move in opposite directions at speeds often compounding diametrically to 150 m.p.h., while spaced only a few horizontal feet apart. No single behavior of man, including his sum total killing during eighty centuries of known warfaring, has taken as great a toll of human lives as has his automobile in its only two-thirds of one century existence. Unheeding potential accidents, hour after hour, day after day, around the clock and around the world, hundreds of millions of human beings hand-guide their automobiles in the lethally dangerous diametric proximity. With common labor now earning three dollars an hour in the United States, and rating humanity's auto driving time at that level, three hundred billion annual dollars' worth of time is being invested by humanity in the nerve-disciplined concentration on death-dodging steering. This concentrated human effort properly directed could produce a more desirable means of getting privately from here to there than by automobile.

The lesson we are being taught by experience is that man does not act with spontaneous wisdom when the gravitationally imposed hazards are not dramatically obvious. On the other hand, he becomes ever more comprehensively responsible and capable as the degree of gravitational hazard is visually evidenced. Suddenly confronted with a precipitous descent of the road, man quickly heeds the highway danger sign to put his car in low gear—although he will speed by a danger sign on horizontal pavement. When his auto tire deflates, however, there is only a four-inch fall—"that's nothing," says man, "I can brake my car swiftly and safely to a roadside stop." It is also the lack of dramatic gravitational hazard that leaves people in trouble parked beside the highway unaided by thousands of passersby. The passerby autoist sees them standing safely on the ground and excuses his nonsolicitude by assuming that some official will soon come along and attend to their needs.

Men in ships traveling at sea behave quite differently from automobilists. With watery depths below, sometimes as great as five miles, humanity is constantly reminded by many dramatic factors that it can fall into the sea at any moment and thence from the rough and hazardous water's surface into the multi-fathomed, lethally suffocating depths. Frequently surfaced with vertically cresting mountainous waves, the sea is gravitationally unforgiving. Consequently, men have designed their ships with continually increasing competence. Men also navigate their ships on a vast almost totally unoccupied surface, instead of within the one-dimensional tubes of the high speed, exclusively linear, land travel. Ships at sea can maneuver in any lateral direction and any two ships in a given vicinity usually allow great distances to separate their respectively steered courses. The fog hazards of sea traffic are great but nowhere nearly so great as are the fog hazards of man traveling diametrically only a few feet apart in the "tubular" highways on dry land.

The ever-present, subconscious hazard-awareness affecting the conceptioning of humans in the design of ships of the sea relates most prominently to the gravitational pull inward toward Earth's center. When a great ship's ends are elevated by two separate mountain waves, the ship acts as a beam between two end supports and the ship's tonnage at center is pulled by gravity with enormous force. When a moment later one great wave supports the ship at midpoint, then gravity reverses the stresses by pulling the cantilevered bow and stern toward the Earth's center. Thus ships get wrecked by ever-alternating stresses as they roll and pitch complexedly. While big buildings on land may and do sometimes, but very rarely, experience the wave motions of earthquakes, the latter are so

120

rare as to have been unanticipated by building designers. Most of the ruination of the great B.C. Greek architecture was caused by centuries-apart earthquakes. Seaquakes occur daily and the designers of ships have to anticipate them. Thus great engineering had its beginning in ships. So great is man's subconscious awareness of gravity as the number one social threat that sailors at sea, distressed by storms, radio-apprised of the lethal dilemma of another crew whose ship is out of control and sinking, will rush to the aid of that sinking ship despite the peril to themselves. Millenniums of sea experiences demonstrate that this vital concern of sailors of all nations for the peril of others on the same sea holds true from the earliest days of wind- and oar-propelled boats to the present days of the great power-driven steel vessels.

Rising in diametric defiance of gravity, sky ballooning engaged the most thoughtfully anticipatory designing competence of scientists. The Chinese in 400 B.C. invented non-man-carrying hot air balloons. Lighter-than-air gas-filled balloons to carry men intrigued inventors for centuries. Anyone familiar with the tediously long task of filling a balloon with gas knows that with even a large rip it takes a very long time for a balloon to deflate, so it always settles gently to the ground. Because strong fabrics could be used and there were no sharp objects in the sky to pierce them, balloons were what is known in engineering as "fail-safe." Balloons obeyed the same principle of *displacement* as that discovered by Archimedes to account for ships floating upon water. When an *enveloped mass* weighs less than the mutable liquid or gaseous medium in which it is immersed, gravity pulls center-of-Earthward so mightily upon the heavier liquid or gaseous medium surrounding the lighter enveloped mass that the latter is emitted vertically outward from Earth's center into the ever-lesser pressures, densities and weight of the Earth's liquid and gaseous oceans until the weight of the locally surrounding air or liquid volume displaced by the *enveloped mass* weighs the same as the latter.

Balloons floating in the atmosphere, like wooden rafts on the sea, had to go where the winds and currents floated them. Seeking favoring winds at different altitudes by alternating dumping either sand or gas, the balloonists could maneuver their spherical vehicles only very meagerly and had to yield to their meanderous driftings. Lacking the threat of unexpectedly swift vertical descent, neither rafts nor balloons excited public apprehension of *fatal falling*. But the airplanes did excite that sense. Airplanes could not float in the air. They were much heavier than the air. They could climb at a gradual angle into the sky but only as their wingfoils were pulled through the air at sufficient speed to produce a negative pressure—or lift— above their wing surfaces. It must be remembered that gasoline engines were notoriously unreliable for many of the automobile's and the airplane's early years. The velocity at which a heavy gasoline engine and its heavy fuel tanks had to pull the wingfoil in order to produce lift was approximately that of a hurricane. Moving such a complex through the air produced enormous drag. All those considerations of the design-scientist-inventor-experimenter meant that the structure must be strong enough to withstand super-to-hurricane and super-to-earthquake stress capabilities yet be light enough to permit the total airframe and power plant ensemble plus the weight of pilot and fuel to be lifted by the wingfoils' maximumly induced lift. The possibility of power plant failure or of a too greatly reduced structural dimension was so great as to invoke not just the pilot's and the engineer's gravity consciousness but also all of humanity's apprehension of the non-restrainable falling by tailspun aviators. So constantly present in everybody's imagination were aviation's early fliers and so constantly conscious was society of the unrelenting gravity peril that every aviator of the early days of airplane flying became known intimately by their names and personalities to vast numbers despite there being at that time no radio—let alone TV—broadcasts. Newspapers published telegraphed and cabled news, but the news network was then so meager as to be able to serve less than one-quarter of humanity. So imaginatively stimulating to society was the gravitational hazard ever-present in heavier-than-air flying that the highest engineering and scientific integrity developed theretofore exclusively by the designers of water-borne vessels was greatly sharpened and spontaneously invested by all concerned in any phase of the production, maintenance and flying of the airplanes. Airplane science introduced not only wind tunnel research but a host of new instrumental measurements of every aspect of strength and power requirements, as well as chemical, physical and mathematical means of providing ever greater performance of all parts and of the whole airplane for each fractional ounce of physical chemistry invested into the complex aircraft organism. It was gravity that the aircraft scientists always struggled most strenuously to overcome. Finally we get to multigravity magnitudes of stress to 3 g's, 4, 5 . . . 8 g stresses to be withstood by ever less g's invested in the power plant and airframes. We even get to "g" suits for the high-speed, high-altitude diving and pull-out pilots themselves.

Without knowing of Galileo's discovery of the accelerating-acceleration progressively compounding the velocity of falling bodies, children dropping objects to the floor and later out of windows and catching high-fly baseballs become intuitively aware of the lethally multiplied speed of falling from ever greater heights. As a consequence, the difference in degree of design-science integrity invested by humanity in its design and production of the only four-inch fallable, blowout experiencing automobiles and the multi-thousand foot fallability of the airplane pilot or passenger is illuminatingly disclosed when we review the relative weights per each developed "horsepower" of the automobile's and the airplane's reciprocating engines—which started with a mutual weight of seven pounds per horsepower at the outset of World War One. Fifteen years later the automobile's engine still weighed seven pounds per horsepower, but the airplane's had been reduced to one pound per horsepower. This reduction in weight, time and energy units invested in each and every function of the aeronautical airframes, power plants and instruments accelerated compoundingly throughout the first sixty years of the airplane to transform it from a vehicle capable of flying only one man, nonstop, for only one mile in one minute at great risk, to an aeronautical vehicle capable of flying three hundred people nonstop across all major oceans at ten miles per minute at far less risk of life—with but one exception—than by any other historically known mode of locomotion per each accomplished mile, including man's walking on dry land. And whereas in his total record of automobiling man has demonstrated his most horrendously lethal record, his total record of flying has proven it to be—with only that one exception—the most spectacularly safe mode of travel known to us. This safety has also been multiplied by the fact that whereas auto traffic is one-dimensional and the ship of the sea two-dimensional, the airplane is three-dimensional and its flight paths are negotiated at great vertical as well as horizontal distances apart. The airport approach zones are also four-dimensional, for the airplanes are separated by controlled time intervals as well as by the other dimensions of space.

What is that one exception in traveling that is safer than the airplane? It is humanity's extraterrestrial space travel. Up to the time I was born average man in his whole lifetime moved to-and-fro about the surface of Earth for an average total of thirty thousand miles. Historically, average man has seen only about one millionth of the surface of his spherical planet Earth. The year I was born the automobiles were born. When I was nine the first airplane was flown. Both modes of travel have multiplied so fast that at seventy-three years of age I have now covered three and one-half million miles around Earth's surface, which is over one hundredfold the average total lifetime travel of those living before us. And I am only one of ten million human beings who have traveled such a distance. Every air hostess is now out-mileaging me to a considerable degree. But each of the Gemini astronauts of a few years ago accomplished my three and one-half million miles in only one week. In the short span of only eight years since Yuri Gagarin became the first Earthian human to travel extraterrestrially, the U.S.A. astronauts, with a group total of approximately two thousand hours of space-travel time—taking off vertically against gravity at a speed two hundred times that of a hurricane's devastating velocity—have traveled in Earth and Moon orbiting terms a total of thirty million miles—without one in-flight loss of life. And, to be realistic, those mileage figures have to be very greatly multiplied because all the while they were orbiting the Earth or the Moon these two great spherical bodies also were flying in formation around the Sun at 60,000 m.p.h. When the astronauts are launched at an additional acceleration of 15,000 m.p.h. to break out of Earth's gravity by speeding 15,000 m.p.h. faster than Earth's 60,000 m.p.h., they are traveling at an independent solar system speed of 75,000 m.p.h., which is just sufficient extra speed to be able to shuttle back and forth between the 60,000 m.p.h. Sun orbiting Moon-Earth, space-vehicle team. This means that the astronauts' two thousand in-space hours have taken them safely

125

through the solar domain a total of one hundred and fifty million miles without one in-flight loss of life and only three preflight deaths.

"Countdown" at Cape Kennedy is not from *ten* to *one*. It is from *ten million* to *one* of tasks that have to be meticulously accomplished in an overall countdown spanning several years —all with such integrity of execution by each of hundreds of thousands of humans participating in the realization of the task that not one fatal flaw has been admitted into the fail-safe designed system.

And so important is the integrity of humanity's investment of its all-time inventory of knowledge and highest mental and physical capability in gravity-mastering, *ergo,* in astro-travel accomplishment, that when three human beings were destroyed before the start of one of its flights, three billion humans around Earth's surface had learned of their deaths in a few minutes and the gravity-invoked imagination of all humanity felt utter anguish for those three unfulfilled astronautical lives. Critical consternation over the total space system's first and only failure was universal—while on the same day around the world three thousand humans died in auto accidents almost unnoticed. Auto-travel is horizontal. Astro-travel is vertical. Those three were trapped in their horizontal to vertical pre-blast-off transitional state. Countdown had not been completed.

And all the while some of our politicians and many tax-abhorring citizens say, "Never mind that space stuff—let's get *down to Earth?* Let's take care of housing the Chinese!" And we reply: *"Where* and *What* is *DOWN TO EARTH?* Where is that nonspace, infinitely extensible only one- and two-dimensional horizontality wherein their out of this world, squarely-reflexing brains percolate—in a *specialization* exonerated, socioeconomic realm of utter irresponsibility for anything but this year's exclusively ego-centered profits?"

In which direction of Universe is DOWN located? Science has found no such region in our celestial events theater. The *UP* and *DOWN* concepts were invented by yesterday's inadequately informed humans to accommodate their concept of a substantially flat and four-cornered Earth to whose unitary, planar, sea-level surface all perpendiculars had, of geometric necessity, to be parallel to one another, wherefore they were all extendable only in two opposite directions—*UP* and *DOWN*. Spherically operating aero-astronautics recognized that none of the perpendiculars to different points on a sphere are parallel to one another; wherefore, separate verticals lead outwardly into space in an infinity of different directions, all of which orientation becomes progressively changed as the Earth sphere spins and orbits and the solar system shifts its galaxy positioning, and our galaxy travels in respect to other revolutions. Aviators have wisely learned to speak of "coming *IN* for a landing" or "going *OUT*" into circumferential flight.

But the public is not so enlightened. The President of the United States, as most typical of societies' geometrical illiteracy, congratulated the 1968 Christmastime astronauts for going *UP,* to, around the Moon and back *DOWN* to Earth; and even scientists still think they "see" the Sun "going down" at twilight. And everybody goes on thinking and talking UP and DOWN unreality. So all humanity's reflexing is as yet so ill-conditioned by years of optical illusion, self-deception and general-education-dispensed misinformation, that it goes right on coddling its own ignorance as well as overwhelming its children with the inventory of formally tolerated errors, thus perpetuating and increasing the polluted information.

In the great Cape Kennedy "countdowns" of ten million uncompleted essential tasks to be reduced to one, then to none, then blast-off—the "critical path" controlling of the complexedly over-lapping, start-to-finish, time-spans of each of the prelaunch tasks to be faultlessly accomplished—99.9 percent of these tasks must be performed within realms of the electromagnetic spectrum, or within dimensional error-control tolerances, which are completely invisible to humanity's naked eye.

When at Christmastime 1968 the Moon-circuiting Earthian astronauts pointed their television camera at the planet Earth and the "live" picture was electromagnetically transmitted at the speed of light (and of all radiation) of 186,000 miles per second, it took the picture approximately two seconds traveling to come into view in our one billion (approximately) Earth-around TV sets. As the planet Earth's cloud-bewreathed, sapphire-watered blueness was dramatically displayed against the x-trillions of time years of nothingness (whose incredible depths appear to us only as pure no-light, a quality of blackness never before experienced), America's senior TV commentator exclaimed, "There she is—floating there!" Floating in what? Man, unable to see the hands of the clock move or the growth motion of a tree or boy, or the motion of the stars, or the atoms, as yet thinks in exclusively static single frames, isolatingly extracted from his scenario Universe. With no recognized scenery behind it, the Earth seemed motionless "back down there."

In *reality,* of course, which anyone will agree is the "practical" way to think, the astronauts were pointing their camera at a third of a million-miles-away Earth from aboard their seventy-five thousand solar-system miles per hour space-speeding vehicle as it circled the 60,000 m.p.h. speeding space vehicle Moon and, together with their space-vehicle-team-mate Earth, all three, Earth, Moon and Cape Kennedy Capsule, zoomed soundlessly, windlessly at a group rate of 60,000 m.p.h. around the Sun—their group mass being tethered co-heringly by the incredibly great gravitational force of our prime energy-supplying space vehicle—the Sun's massiveness.

Because Universe and its inexorable evolutionary scenario operates everywhere under utterly invisible rules that are 99.9 percent unsensed and unheeded by man, his yesterday's inventory of exclusively "sensible" behaviors is disclosed as being approximately irrelevant to scenario—evolution's real "shooting script," and the heedlessness fortunately has been, thus far, approximately innocuous to Universe. If the irrelevance and misinformation persist, however, and are further multiplied, they are destined to bring about lethal malfunctioning of the complement of human passengers that evolution placed —separately and experimentally—aboard our almost negligible-in-Universe-sized, space vehicle Earth.

Space vehicle Earth was so superbly well designed, equipped and supplied as to have been able to sustain human life aboard it for at least two million years—despite humanity's comprehensive ignorance which permitted a fearfully opinionated assumption of an infinitely extensive planar *World*. Humanity also spontaneously misassumed that its local pollution could be dispelled by the world's infinite extensiveness. Humanity also misassumed that an infinite succession of new and pleasing varieties of abundant, vital resources would be disclosed progressively as man exhausted first one and bespoiled another of the as yet known valuable, because vital, resources. Man must learn in a spontaneously self-enlightening manner to discard many, if not most, of yesterday's false premises, and axioms only believingly accepted; and he must, on his own, discard false premises and learn that only the non-sense Universe is reliable and that a lunatic is not a crazy man but one so sane, well informed, well coordinated, self-disciplined, cooperative and fearless as to be the first Earthian

129

human to have been ferried to a physical landing upon the Moon and thereafter to have returned safely to reboard his mother space vehicle "Earth."

Long, long ago—little bands of humans seeking fish and fruits, or following animals, frequently became permanently lost and separated from one another. Endowed with the procreative urge, those of the few males and females surviving in company inbred for generations in their respective remotenesses utterly unaware of one another's tribes and separate tribal evolution—and thus evolved a plurality of superficial differences in appearance through special chromosomic concentration brought about by the special characteristics of the survival adaptation process. Thus have developed hundreds of only superficially different human types, some very numerous and powerful, some successfully monopolizing specific land areas and others as yet wandering. In their ignorance, all of humanity's national governments assume, misinformedly, that there is not and never will be enough of the vital resources to support all or even a large number of humans, *ergo,* that they must automatically fight one another to the death to discover which government might survive. Often to encourage their respective peoples, political leaders evolve partly expedient and partly idealistic ideologies suitable to their viewpoints, but all the ideologies misassume an only-you-or-me—not both—survival premise as having no axiomatic alternative. Because of the invisibility of 99.9 percent of the source information that contradicts the assumption of a fundamental inadequacy of resources, the probability is that if man is left exclusively to political contriving, he will become embroiled in approximately total self-destruction. While the top speed of the intercontinental ballistic rocket is many times that of a bullet, its 20,000 m.p.h. is as nothing beside radar-sight's speed of 70,000,000 m.p.h. The speed of information is now so swift that for the first time in history the lethal missile is no longer faster than man's ability to apprehend both its coming and its specific course—twenty minutes before it can reach him. But the ability to see it coming does not confer the capability to dodge it. Now every one of the opposed political systems' swiftest rocketry attacks can be detected so far in advance that each and every side can dispatch, retaliatorily, not only its full arsenal of atomic warheads but also all its rocket-borne chemical and biological warfare missiles. All opposed sides can and will retaliate automatically *in toto,* thus bringing about approximately total human destruction of vast millions immediately, with the balance to be destroyed soon thereafter by the radiational, biological and chemical contamination.

Shifting abruptly from consideration of such a negative conclusion and seeking to understand some of the alternative options to such a fate, let us select any two averagely healthy and well-dispositioned young men from among the world's professional airplane-flying and maintenance population. One of the two we will select from among those licensed airplane pilots who have not only qualified to fly their own, land and sea, single and dual engined aircraft but also have gone on to get both their *commercial* and *flying instructor* licenses. The other young man selected will be from among the airport personnel who have qualified under United States regulations to be licensed as an airframe or power plant mechanic. Let us follow through intimately the behavior patterns of both the flying instructor and the mechanic at work and during off-duty waking hours. We find the instructor at work with a student flyer, behaving with the utmost integrity of which he is capable, having in common with all such instructors an overwhelming and spontaneously induced subconscious awareness of the split-second span of time within which a non-correctable error or situation leading to fatality—if not understood and instantly corrected—could be inadvertently initiated by the student, which could lead to the fearfully imaginable vertical acceleration by gravity inward toward Earth and almost certain death. The airframe or power plant mechanic working on an airplane we find to be inspired by the same imagination-vivified awareness of the fatal predicament of the flyer, were he, the mechanic, to fail to perform his maintenance and repair tasks in the most experience-proven and safety-guaranteeing manner. When the airplane maintenance mechanic certifies in writing, as is routinely required, that he has performed any given structural, mechanical, repair, tuning or testing task, his certification is as reliable as (if not inherently more so than) certification by a great surgeon that he, the surgeon, has performed any given physiological operation. The surgeon cannot certify, as can the mechanic, that the system he has operated on, if supplied with routine fuels and handling, will operate reliably for a given period of forward time. There is far more opinion and guess work residual in the human surgery arts than in aeronautical technology.

But let our average flying instructor and his friend the average airplane mechanic check out from the airport and ride into town together in one of their automobiles and their behavioral integrity begins to fall off. One is liable to mutter to the other that the driver of another car who crowded his way is the offspring of a dog, to which the other agrees—although both know that this is biologically impossible. The same mechanic working for an automobile service station may perform a sloppy job or leave some job unattended, for he envisions at worst the auto driver's stopping unexpectedly and having to push his car to the roadside.

Measurable data concerning the relative reliability of the human factors operative throughout the almost *horizontal* (and often glide-recoverable) aeronautical arts—compared with those comprehensively operative throughout the *vertical,* non-glidable, approximately zero-recovery potential art and service of astro-rocketed human travel—disclose a multifold step-up of inherent integrity of spontaneous behavior, as well as of intellectual integrity, of the comprehensively anticipatory design science with which its every undertaking is initiated and maintained, both throughout and retrospectively of every such undertaking. This super-to-previous level of integrity holds true throughout the whole air-space industry's production and delivery of every item of equipment. It is operative in equal degree of relative perfection of behavior and knowledge to that invested in the selection and training of the astronauts, as well as in the launching, flight, control, and advance research design and general administration.

The spontaneous advance of both metaphysical and physical integrity of the astro-art over the already magnificent aeronautical science and technology is inherent in the nature of the minimum standards within either aero-flight or space-flight that could be attained and maintained.

Heisenberg's principle of "indeterminism" prohibits any *exact* measurement or "absolutely exact" physical agreement of mechanical or structural fitting. As a consequence, engineering and mechanics can only *reduce* the degree of error to be tolerated. Scientists must be content with "relatively elegant agreements." "All the truth and nothing but the truth," as pledged under imposed oath-giving in courts of justice in many countries, is vainly pledged, for, contrary to indeterminism, absolute "truth" is assumed to be legally demonstrable in the eyes of the administrators of humanly invented law. Detection of any natural aberration, witting or unwitting, may bring prosecution and conviction for false testimony. For a long time mechanics have known what Heisenberg—and science through him—so recently discovered to be true: that Universe forbids realization of *exactitude*. The Heisenberg indeterminism implies *eternity* to be persistent within the physical and metaphysical, ever-evolving, continuity-finiteness of scenario universe, in which the myriads of nonsimultaneously shaken kaleidoscopes are never either simultaneous or identically repetitious. Having both the *finiteness* discovered by modern physics as well as *eternity* imposes a limitless change, *ergo,* a never repeating and irreversible omnievolution. Although he had never heard of Heisenberg, the skilled machinist could see long ago that the best he could do was to reduce the amount of error he might tolerate and with very surprisingly desirable results.

For instance, when we reduce the tolerance of error in the relative exactitude of the manufacturer's sizing of individual rivet diameters and of the interpositioning of the holes and the diameter of the holes that are to receive the rivets, with which two metal sheets are to be drawn together to act as one structural piece, the strength of the integral assembly, provided by the riveting, increases rapidly. The human hand guided only by the human eye, unaided by a magnifying glass, cannot interposition the centers of a plurality of rivet holes or visibly discern the magnitude of the spaces lying between the holes, nor observe and thereby control the diameter sizing of the holes to a degree finer than $1/100$ of an inch. By the use of instruments and mechanical tools, such hole interpositioning and diameter dimensioning can be held to a tolerance of error of less than $1/10,000$ of an inch in airplane fabrication and assembly work. In the electromagnetically monitored astronautical technology, however, the error tolerances are often reduced to a reliability within $1/1,000,000$ of an inch. Using only the automobile industry's relatively crude tool-making tolerances and *reducing* the degree of error to be tolerated from that of

134

the best skilled metalworker's naked-eye layout work, of 1/100 of an inch, to a machine-tool-controlled 1/1000 of an inch, I was able to gain much strength increase in the riveted assembly of an aluminum structured ninety-three-foot diameter geodesic dome, to cover the Court of the Ford Motor Company's Dearborn, Michigan, Rotunda Building in 1952. Thereby I was able to produce and install a dome weighing only one-half as much as would the lightest dome of equal strength that could have been produced and assembled at that time—even by a team of history's most skilled sheet metal workers, if they were confined to operating only with the optimum naked-eye tolerance-discerning capability. This is to say that automated, industrial, mass-production controls could produce *two* domes, of equal strength and quality, for every *one* that could be turned out by the best craft manufacturing techniques, and thirty domes for each that could be produced by the tolerance of our present building business. When we *millionfold* the degree of accuracy, the strength and reliability are multiplied to an even more important degree. The astro-vehicle technology operates at so phenomenal an increase of performance per pound of engine and fuel consumed as compared to airplanes, which in themselves are not only sometimes thousandsfold more efficient than automobiles in accomplishing man-miles per units of invested physical resource, that it makes *possible* doing what it was *impossible* for the lesser art *to do at all*. The rocket can go to the Moon whereas the airplane cannot, and the airplane can cross the ocean under its own independent power and controls, which an automobile cannot.

Whereas in the mechanics and structures of autos and airplanes the physical principles employed and the intertiming of cycles are conceptually comprehensible, in the electromagnetic world, where the activity speed is stepped up to seven

135

hundred million miles an hour (which is thirty-five thousand times faster than the fastest rocket, three hundred and fifty thousand times faster than the fastest airplane and three and one-half million times faster than the fastest automobile), the scientific explorer-inventor has no visualizable concept of how nature does what gets done. In electronics, the designer does his circuitry layout work mathematically, and all opinionated decisions give way to mathematical integrity. In the astro-vehicle technology, dial-read electromagnetically levered needle movements, rather than physical size gauges, take over, and the mathematics of the entirely invisible process-controls are derived from electromagnetically operated computers whose reliability is provided by the invisible, but fantastically reliable, circuitry behaviors of the self-interstructuring and invisible transaction atoms.

In coordinating the ten-million-to-none order of magnitude reduction of essential tasks to be pre-accomplished before each blast-off at Cape Kennedy, a whole new era of industrial intercourse integrity has been established. As a happy but popularly unrealized consequence a new and large section of our economic system has been elevated to an entirely new level of incorruptible reliability. (This is the level of integrity manifest today in our high school youth.) Hence we see the passenger-miles safely accomplished per each pound of astro-engine as well as by each ounce of astro-fuel, ten thousandfold over the airplane's and its fuel's best performance. To demonstrate this fantastic improvement in performance, we witness that one communications-relaying satellite of only one quarter of one ton of material is now outperforming the transoceanic communications message capacity and fidelity capability of 175,000 tons of copper cable. This constitutes a seven hundred thousandfold step-up in communications performance per pound of invested resources. And don't forget that we were already favorably impressed with the sevenfold increase of horsepower per pound accomplished by the manufacturers of the light private-airplane engine over the pounds per horsepower of the auto engine.

As in our industrio-social age we now design everything *except* the astro-vehicle paraphernalia, all the metals that have ever been mined and put to use have an average quarter century recycling, invention-to-obsolescence periodicity which includes the scrap, melt, redesign and re-use cycling time. All the metals ever mined and so put to use are now invested in structures and machines that, if operated at full capacity, could take care of only forty-four percent of humanity. The rate at which we have been finding and mining new metals is far slower than the rate of increase of human population. This means that if we freeze the world's design standards at their present levels, which are far below the standards of the astro-vehicle technology, fifty-six percent of humanity, which means humanity's political majority, is doomed to premature demise, and to want and suffering enroute to that early death. There is nothing that politics, per se, can do to alter that condition; only a design revolution—such as that which is already "made to order" in the potentially thousandfold performance per pounds, minutes and kilowatts advancement to be realized by the astro-vehicle industry—can change those fundamental conditions of humanity overnight from failure to comprehensive world-around, human success.

Between 1900 and 1969 our space vehicle Earth's passengers have experienced an increase of from less than one percent of its total population to forty-one percent of total world population now enjoying a standard of living superior to that either experienced or dreamed of by any monarch before 1900. During that time the material resources per each world man were continually decreasing so that the advancement was not accomplished by exploiting more resources. This historical forty-folding of the percentage of humanity's "haves" can only be explained as the fall-out of ever higher performance per pound technology as developed for the ships of the world's water and air oceans. That an overnight advancement from forty to one hundred percent is possible can be understood when we realize that the technological fall-out into our domestic economy of ships of extraterrestrial astrogation have not had time to have important effect on the standard of living because their technological fall-out has not yet had time to occur.

We have discovered that the higher the speed and the more angularly contradictory to gravity humanity's communicating facilities have become, the higher the integrity of total thinking, as well as behavior, and the higher the performance realized per each unit of resource invested. At the bottom of the technological ladder lies the massive, inert, superstition-corruption-misery-and-strife-ridden, subindustrial, craft-and-graft building activity. No architect, let alone the public and its politicians (who keep their real estate, bank and construction interests rolling along with government financed inefficiency), has the slightest idea what buildings weigh, yet without such weight knowledge humanity cannot possibly start providing more housing with less resources, thereby ultimately to take care of everybody and thus eliminate the fundamental cause of war, which all youth now intuits could be done if the grown-ups would get their sights elevated and forsake preoccupation with this year's profits, this year's election and each with his own special survival intrigues. If the myopia were dispensed with and the whole of humanity were to become cooperatively engaged in learning realistically that we *are* aboard a space vehicle that is not going to get any new equipment yet could be operated successfully for all, we would have to allow the space program to continue and also to accredit it above all other officially sponsored and financed activity. If on the other hand we were to heed the tax-itchy "down to earther" and confine ourselves to trying to "house the Chinese," as he puts it, we would soon find that his idea of housing couldn't be stretched to take care of the ill-housed balance of humanity. Since the "down to earther" doesn't know how much houses weigh, he obviously does not know what he is talking about. The kinds of pipes and sewers he now thinks of as constituting adequate housing can't be stretched to accommodate fifty percent of humanity, let alone his disdainfully referred to "Chinese."

While no scientist has ever been retained by any patron to look at the plumbing, no improvement other than colored plumbing fixtures has been realized in the last five thousand years in our five-gallons-to-get-rid-of-one-pint systems for shunting rivers through our toilets and sewers and thence back into our ever more polluted water-supply streams.

Shifting our attention for the moment from our urgent urbanism, we realize that, in order to have humans live for any protracted period of time in space where there are no streams or sewers in which to flush, nor air to be breathed, nor gardens, nor fish, nor fruit to be eaten, the problems to be solved are far greater than those already frustrating our Earthbound living. To maintain men in space, with four billion people watching them constantly over the soon to be completed world-around satellite relaying communications system, without invoking the consternation and dismay of all humanity, we are going to have to learn, for the first time, all about the chemistry, physics, ecology and metabolics of the total life-regenerating system of our space vehicle Earth. We are going to have to learn how to pack into a little portable electrochemical system about the size and weight of one large air-travel suit-

139

case all the life-supporting technology necessary to complement man's integral organic processing, with possibly an additional weekly milk bottle-full of metabolic essentials rocketed to each astronaut from his mother-spacecraft Earth. When and if humanity learns how to support human life successfully *anywhere in Universe,* the logistical economics of doing so will become so inherently efficient and satisfactory that then, and then alone, we may for the first time make all humanity a success back here aboard our space vehicle Earth. The U.S.A. and U.S.S.R. have each appropriated multibillions toward accomplishment of this task. The United states has already had an experimental team operating successfully under semiautonomous conditions in a simulation operation lasting successfully for more than one whole year in such isolation. When that actual, protracted, semiautonomous living has been accomplished in space, the prototype apparatus may easily have cost the United States and Russia a combined fifteen billion dollars. But that fifteen billion dollar prototype can then be mass-reproduced and distributed on board Earth at a cost per person of only a few dollars a year while doing away with sewers, waterlines and approximately all pollution.

Among the most difficult administrative tasks the U. S. Space Administration experienced in initiating the first Cape Canaveral (now Cape Kennedy) space-vehicle launching was the problem of the over-zealousness of its dedicated and inspired scientists and engineers who weren't "going to leave it to the machine to get things done right"—they had to "do it themselves." But these over-dedicated individuals couldn't possibly operate with their senses and muscles at the magnitudes of precision and velocity essential to the invisible coordination of the computer-monitored electromagnetic relay systems. *All those involved in the space program* had to be convinced that the only place and time in which their personally disciplined options of thought and action could be safely engaged were in improving the original reliability of each and every item that went into the complexedly automated system. They must concentrate anticipatorily in the design, production and installation of the basic tools and leave it to the tools to do man's comprehensive bidding.

It seems eminently clear that we not only must put our space programs on highest priority of attention and resource investment but that all humanity must be accredited and financed to enter into a new re-educational system that is geared to develop our most prominent awareness, that we indeed *are in space* and that all of our concern is with the fact that our space vehicle Earth and its life-energy-giving Sun, and the tide-pumping Moon can provide ample sustenance and power for all humanity's needs to be derived from our direct energy income without further robbing our fossil fuels energy savings account. In reality, the Sun, the Earth and the Moon are nothing else than a most fantastically well-designed and space-programed team of vehicles. All of us *are,* always *have been,* and so long as we exist, *always will be—nothing else but—astronauts.* Let's pull our heads out of the brain benumbing, mind frustrating, misinformedly conditioned reflexes. If it is going to be "All ashore who's going ashore," once more intent to return to nonspace DOWN HERE ON EARTH, humanity is doomed.

But there is hope in sight. The young! While the university students are intuitively skeptical of the validity of any and all evolution-blocking establishments, *ergo,* negatives, the high school age youth thinks spontaneously and positively in astro- and electromagnetic technology and their realistic uses. The young of all age levels abhor hypocrisy. They are bored with obsolete UP and DOWN dancing, with bureaucratic inertia, bias of any kind or fear-built security. They disdain white,

141

gray, black and blue lies. The students and school children around the world have idealistic compassion for all humanity. There is a good possibility that they may take over and successfully operate SPACESHIP EARTH.

# GO IN TO GO OUT

## GO IN TO GO OUT

Lying in the outskirts
Of St. Louis, Missouri, U.S.A.
The Edwardsville Religious Center
Of Southern Illinois University
Stands with surveyor-certified mathematical exactitude
Symmetrically astride the true planet Earth's
"90th"
Western meridian of longitude.

The 40-foot diameter three-quarter sphere dome
Of the Religious Center
Is a transparent miniature Earth.
Our planet's continents can be seen
Accurately outlined against the transparent blue oceans
As they would be seen by X rays
If one descended by elevator from Edwardsville
To the center of the real Earth
Always keeping Edwardsville directly overhead.
The continental shapes appear reversed
But soon become as easy to read as mirrored images.

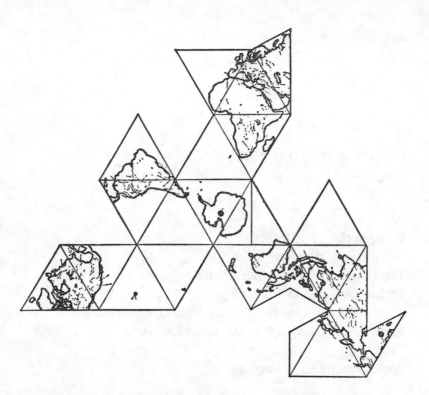

WORLD I—WATER OCEAN: *Population areas are concentrated along the outermost blades of the continental propeller presenting the centrifugal pattern with no traffic at all at the Antarctic center. Half of humanity is in India and China (Kipling's "East"), 28 per cent in Europe (the "Far West"), 10 per cent in Africa, and 12 per cent in the Americas.*

The *miniature Earth* dome's "90th" meridian *West*
And the *real Earth's* "90th" meridian *West*
And their respective North-South polar axes,
As well as Lhasa, Tibet, Bangladesh, and Calcutta
On the real Earth's "90th" meridian *East,*
All lie in exactly the same geometrical plane
Which vertically cleaves the tangent

146

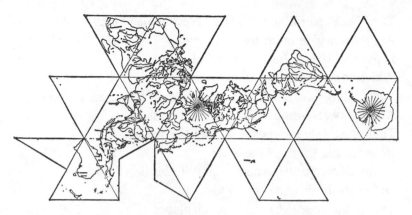

WORLD II—AIR OCEAN: *The continents are assembled around the land mass instead of around the water mass. Ninety per cent of humanity can reach one another on the shortest great circle air routes without going near the oceans.*

Edwardsville Miniature and the real Earth spheres.
All the polar great circles'
East-West meridional degree completions add to 180°
"80" West continues beyond the poles as "100" East
However only "90" West continues as "90" East
And can be referred to combinedly as *the* "90th."

The "90th" runs through the demographic center
Not only of North America's 9 per cent of humanity,
But also through the integrated demographic center
Of Russia and the Orient's 60 per cent of humanity.
Look north along the "90th" to two-thirds of all humanity.
Look north and south along "90" to all humanity
Existing less than five jet hours distance,
Away overland from the "90th."
The "90th" is our planet's great circle mainstreet.

The "90th" meridian's East and West hemispheres
Are those which uniquely identified
Kipling's "East is East, and West is West,"
Which "twain" he said, shall "never meet."
But Kipling was thinking only of East-West ocean voyaging
And the twelve-thousand watery miles distance
That seemingly interposed six months' travel
Between the East and the West
As an insurmountable human multitudes barrier
Only two-thirds of a century ago.
During the year 1961, three jet airplanes
Carried more passengers across the Atlantic
Than did the *Queen Mary*
In one-tenth of the crossing time
And at a competitively devastating cost reduction.

East-West, world oceans' surface, passenger transportation
Became obsolete overnight.
And with it withered all its East-West transcontinental
Harbor-to-harbor railway interlinkage
As well as the transient travel and commerce significance
Of all the world's great harbor cities.
This economic demise of the world's harbor cities
Remains for the moment unrecognized because hidden
By the convention and amusement industries' momentum
And far more importantly by the farm-into-cities migration
Of the farm machinery displaced three-quarters of humanity
Who until yesterday lived on and worked the world's farms.

But now flying the "90th" over the North Pole
Ninety per cent of humanity can reach each other in half a day
On the shortest great circle air routes
Without going near the Atlantic, Pacific, or Indian oceans.

Suddenly, the world's oceans' tortuous surfaces
Have become obsolete as the prime human intercourse
    medium.
Awareness of this brings us abruptly
To other epochal realizations such as discovery
That in order to accomplish the now feasible task
Of supporting all humanity at a sustained level
That will permit every living being
And all generations of them to come
Mutually and successfully to enjoy all the Earth—
Without depleting and despoiling resources
And without any human's profiting at the expense of others,
And without onerous interferences
With one another's complex interpatternings
Of individual freedoms and initiatives—
Vast quantities of extra-terrestrially emanating power
Must be harnessed and safely distributed
Around our Earth planet.
This vast energy is needed
To actuate the additional bio-industrial
Metabolic regeneration technology
Now eminently feasible, but not yet accomplished
By the Earthians' design revolution,
The realization of which total physical success
Is now mandatory upon humanity
If it is not only to survive
But is also to fulfill its cosmic function
As consciously competent and majorly responsible participants
In local Universe's regenerative problems solving.

To accomplish the bio-industrial metabolic regeneration
While maintaining chemical balance in terrestrial ecology,
While also accomplishing that system's energy distribution,

There is no way of transporting large quantities of energy
From here to there so swiftly and safely
As by ultra-high-voltage underground electrical networks.
By comparison with the energy transporting capability
Of ultra-high-voltage, long-distance,
Superconductive, underground electric power transmission
Inaugurated and developed since 1961,
Pipelines, supertankers, railway gondolas
Are snail-rate pygmies, ergo economically obsolete.
The "90th" meridian is also central to the North-South
Transarctic electric energy network integration
Of the world's people and their continents,
Which will be accomplished first via Bering Strait
And later by Arctic Ocean-bottom cables
And later yet by beaming techniques.

The "90th's" North and South broad skyway
Not only obsoletes the ages-long East-West travel,
But it also inherently integrates humanity
Even as humanity was heretofore mutually remote
And inherently divided against itself by the oceans.

Equally obsolete to the physical east-westing traffic
Is the metaphysical practice of universal specialization
Which characterizes not only all education
But all business and bureaucracy as well.
Specialization, unlike geographical isolation,
Was arbitrarily imposed and humanly aggravated
By the "divide-and-conquer" strategy
Paramount to the armed monarchs of yesterday.
Specialization was imposed by the monarchs
Upon the 90 per cent illiterate world population
To facilitate the monarch's or ruling minority's

Minding everybody's business, at large,
While forcing all others subserviently
To mind their own individual business, at small,
Thus guaranteeing a general blindfolding of society
Where the ruling minority's own ambitions were to be
    gratified
Only at the (slow or swift) mortal expense of the uninformed
    many.


In the "90th's" East-West to North-South reorientation of
    humanity
Evolution unexpectedly accomplishes
Both the mutual inter-advantaging of all humanity
And its emancipation from its inherently self-divided
East-West remoteness and selfishly emphatic history.
This reorientation revolves centrally about
The educational revolution of young world society
Which is rejecting specialization while intuitively cultivating
Its long dormant, innate synergetic comprehensions
Of eternal generalized principles transcendentally governing
The omni-inter-relevancy of all experiential phenomena
Which invisible metaphysical revolution
Is epochally abetted by the invisible electro-magnetic
    revolution
In self-educative electronic search and retrieval of relevant
    video documentaries
All of which non-violent revolution will eventuate in
    spontaneous universal cooperation
Self-started by the common realization of the feasibility of
    total human success
And its obviously sequitur peaceful acquisition procedures.
Returning to the knowledge to be gained from it

We find the miniature Earth's axis is exactly parallel to the
    real Earth's
And the precise center of the Edwardsville miniature Earth
Is only four thousand miles from the real Earth's center.
This distance is astronomically negligible
Being less than one-billionth of the distance
To our nearest star beyond the Sun.
When standing on the mobile observation platform
With eyes at the marked center
Of the miniature Earth's North-South axis
The true celestial North star will be seen on a clear night
Shining brightly at the miniature Earth's north pole center
And looking outwardly through the dome's transparent shell,
Any stars seen at any location on any of the continents or
    oceans
Are at that moment *exactly* in zenith
Over those very geographical points on the real Earth—
Which can be verified instantly by long-distance telephone.
The Religious Center's dome is a true planetarium.

A sense of orientation of each human individual
Within the profound magnificence of Universe
Is provided by the Religious Center's miniature Earth.
One goes inside to go outside one's self
And into the center of the Earth
And thence outward to the stars in seconds.

The Edwardsville Religious Center becomes at once
The cathedral of universal reality
And cathedral of universal mystery
In which is simultaneously revealed
The macro-micro designing integrity
Whose infinitely inclusive, detailed, and tireless

Concern and competence are o'erwhelming manifests
Of the eternal, timeless, cosmically regenerative,
Love-intellect governance of Universe
Which inherently transcends human comprehension
Because of the infinitesimally limited
Locally and myopically over-emphatic experience inventory
Always inadequately informing human consciousness and
    reason.

Einstein said, "What a faith in the orderliness of
    Universe
Must have inspired Kepler
To spend the nights of his life alone with the stars,"
Which inadvertently revealed Einstein's own faith
And that of the billions before him
In the integrity of Universe
Which has ever inspired humans
To commit themselves in all-out love,
Hopeful thereby of increasing human understanding
Of the a priori mystery
Of the ever comprehensively embracing
Yet micro-cosmically permeating
Omni-exquisitely concerned
Eternal Integrity.

# TELEGRAM TO
# SENATOR EDMUND MUSKIE

# TELEGRAM TO
# SENATOR EDMUND MUSKIE

There is dawning world-around comprehension
Of the existence of a significant plurality
Of alternative energy source options
Available for all Earthians' vital support,
Which now intuitively fortifies
Maine's far-sighted citizens' and friends'
Spontaneous expression of abhorrence
For any petroleum refineries or storage
Anywhere along its complexedly meandering
Deep-tide coastline.
Because humanity is born
Helpless, ignorant and naked
Nature must anticipatorily provide,
Protect and nurture humanity's regeneration
By spontaneously assimilatible
Environmental resource availabilities
Under omni-favorable conditions.

But originally permitted ignorance
No longer may be, self-excusingly, pleaded
As justification for failure to employ

The now known to exist
Omni-self-supporting technical capabilities
To produce unprecedentedly advanced
Standards of living
And freedoms of thought and actions
For all humanity,
Without any individual
Being advantaged
At the expense of another,
All of which feasibilities
Are inanimately powerable
Well within our daily energy income
From extraterrestrial sources
And all accomplishable without pollution.

By tapping the billion years' long
Safe-depositing of fossil fuel energies,—
As petroleum and coal, within the planetary crust
Humanity was self-startered
Into inauguration of world-around
Electromagnetic energy resources integration,
Accomplished exclusively
By industrialization's ever-evolving knowledge
Regarding ultimate feasibility
On non-biologically harvested
Metabolic support of all humanity.

Humanity had to be self-startered
Into bounteously underwritten
Trial and error gropings
From whence gradually emerged
Mind-discovered comprehension
Of some of the eternal principles

Governing the availability and feasible employment
Of cosmically-constant, astronomical qualities
Of inherently inexhaustible energies
Of self-regenerative Universe.

Because humanity now has learned
How to gear directly into the inexhaustible energy
Of the main engines of Universe
It is no longer justified in attempting
To accommodate its ever-expanding,
Knowledgeable functioning in Universe
By ignorantly keeping its foot on the self-starter
To obtain its evolutionary propulsion
*Only* from the swiftly exhaustible
Fossil-fuel storage battery energies
Or from its perishable, one-season crops.

Realistic accounting
Of the time and foot pounds
Of energy-work, invested by nature,
In the land-born agriculture's—
And seaborn algae's
Impoundment of Sun energy,—
Exclusively by photosynthesis,—
And its progressive conservation
As dead organic residues progressively covered
By wind and waterborne dustings
Siftings and siltings buried and sunken
To critical, gravitationally actuated,
Pressure depths and temperatures
Within which unique conditions
The hydrocarbon residues are chemically converted
Into coal and petroleum,

159

Discloses an overall time and pressure
Energy accounting cost
Of one million dollars per gallon of petroleum
(Or its energy equivalents in coal)
As calculated at the present
Lowest commercial rates
At which kilowatt hours of energy
May be purchased from public utility systems.

Failure thus to reckon
The fundamental metabolic costs,
Is to be economically reckless.
Further reckless expenditures
Of our fossil fuel energy savings account
To which future generations
Needs must have emergency access
As a self-re-startering recourse,
Is equivalent to drilling a hole
From the sidewalk into a bank vault
Pumping out money
And calling it free-enterprise discovery
Of an energy wealth bonanza.
Physical energy convergent as matter
Or divergent as radiation,
Compounded by weightless metaphysical know-how,
Have altogether provided the means
For Earthians' progressively greater participation
In Universe's inexorable evolutionary transformings,
The participation being accomplished exclusively
By Human-intellect directed ingenuities,
In progressive rearranging
Of the physical furnishings
Of our spherical, space-boat home,

In such a way as progressively to support
Ever-more lives in ever-more ways
With ever-increasing health.

Naught gets *spent* but human time
As cosmically inexhaustible energy
Is tapped exclusively
By intellect-discovered and employed
Cosmic principles
Which to qualify as principles
Must be eternal.

Real wealth
Is Universally self-generative energy
Harnessed by mind to regenerate
Human lives around our Planet,—
Increasing wealth means
More regeneratively self-supporting days ahead
For more lives
Ranging first within Earth's biosphere
And subsequently by ever-increasing exploration
Within Earth's extra-terrestrial
Cosmic neighborhoods.

Such ever-evolving greater know-how wealth
Provides the means
With which specifically to augment
The ever-expanding, anti-entropic
Intellectual responsibilities of humanity
As local Universe's local problem solver
Which problem solving is human intellect's exclusive,
Complementary and essential functioning,
In support of total, scenario-Universe's
Self-regenerative integrity.

Physics shows
That universal energy is undiminishable.
Experience teaches
That every time humanity initiates
Intelligibly logical experiments
Human intellect always learns more.
Intellect cannot learn less
Intellect is growthfully irreversible.
Both the physical and metaphysical advantage gains
Of intelligently harvested know-how,—
Reinvested as competent energy-transforming,—
Always produces
Inherently irreversible wealth growth.

This is contrary to yesterday's
Now scientifically and technically obsolete
Concept of a self-exhausting,
Ergo, progressively expendable—
And ultimately spent Universe,
With assumedly progressive failure phases
And their negative economic accountings
Whose bankruptcies are as yet employed
By all political economies,
Together with their depletion tax evasions
Covering only physical property depletions
With no capitalization, nor depreciation allowances
Of the metaphysical competence of humanity's mind
Without which there would be
Neither human life self-awareness
Nor its wealth
Of capable conceptioning.

Modern physics renders it incontrovertible
That celestial energy is nonexhaustible
Only the fossil fuel savings account
And perishable human muscles
And the self-startering, but limited,
Hydro-carbon impounded energies
Are terrestrially exhaustible.
Humanity's economics are as yet ignorantly geared
Exclusively to the annual energy harvesting cycles
And bankruptcy accounting
Of ignorance permeated yesteryear's
Human brain reflexing
As conditioned, by floods, fires, droughts and pestilence,—
And frequently ruined crops,
Whereby millions of humans perished.

Brilliant and potentially effective
Managerial capabilities and leadership potentials
Are as yet diminishingly extruded
Through minuscule accounting and customs apertures,
Which force those capabilities
To concentrate exclusively and myopically
Only upon *this* year's production
*This* year's election and
*This* year's profit
While blindly overlooking
The infinitely reliable cyclic frequencies
Governing the 99 per cent of reality
Lying outside human sense apprehending
And lying outside this year's considerability
Which vast, invisible reality
Is the great electromagnetic spectrum
And its astrophysical event recurrence rates,

Which range from split-second atomic frequencies
To multi-billion year astro-physical lags
All of which cyclic event reoccurrences
Are guaranteed to humanity as absolutely reliable
By the exclusively science-discovered
Cosmic behaviors' integrity.

Despite the industrial revolution's
Momentary fumbling and mess—
As occasioned uniquely by the myopia
Generated by "this year's accounting" limitations—
It now is discernible scientifically—
That unwitting Earthians
Gradually are being shifted
Over an epochal threshold,
Successful crossing of which,—
If not totally frustrated by reflexive inertias,—
Will witness the successful gearing of all humanity
Into the eternally inexhaustible, energy system
Of omni-self-regenerative celestial mechanics.

Humanity is as yet acquiring
Its many human support increasing
Techniques and practices
For all the wrong reasons.
We only expand wealth production
Under mass-fear mandates of war.
We could acquire, peacefully and directly
A total humanity supporting productivity
And comprehensive enjoyment of our whole planet
By simply deciding to do so.
Whatever we need to do
And know how to do

We can afford to do!
This is the cosmic law
Now in clear scientific evidence,
And the more love,
The more satisfactory the wealth augmentations.
Whether history entrusts you or others
With progressively greater responsibilities
At this crucial-to-Earthians'-survival moment
Depends upon whether you, they, or both of you
Comprehend these epochal transitional events.

The State of Maine's Bay-of-Fundy's
Twice-a-day, fifty-foot tides
Are pulsated by Sun-compensated, Moon-pulls,
Those tides will be pulsated twice daily
As long as the Moon and Earth co-orbit the Sun,
Fundy provides more economically harvestable,
Foot-pounds of energy daily
Than ever will be needed by all humanity
While attaining and sustaining ever-higher
Standards of living,
Greater and more healthful longevity
Than heretofore ever experienced.

It is economic ignorance of the lowest order
To persist in further surfacing and expenditure
Of the Earth's fossil fuels—
It is even more ignorant and irresponsible
To surface and transport oils
Of Arabia, Venezuela, Africa and East Indies
To refineries and storages on the coast of Maine
Thus putting into ecological jeopardy
One of the world's

As yet most humanly cherished
Multi-islanded, sea coast wildernesses.
In view of Fundy's tidal energy wealth
Such blindness is more preposterous
Than "carrying coals to Newcastle."
It is accelerated human suicide.

On the other hand we must recall
That Passamaquoddy's semi-completed
Tidal generating system
Was abandoned on the officially stated,
Ignorant, political-economics assumption
That electricity could not be transmitted
Beyond 350 miles
And therefore could not reach
Any important industrial centers.
It is known in political actuality
That Passamaquoddy was discontinued
Through the combined lobbying efforts
Of Maine's paper pulping and electric power industries
Whose political policy logic was persuasive
Despite that those two industries
Have together succeeded
In polluting Maine's prime rivers
To kill all but a pittance
Of the Maine coast's once vast fishing wealth.

Space-effort harvested
Scientific know-how and the computer capability
Have together made possible
The present inauguration
Of one million volt transmissions
And a 1,500 mile delivery range

Of underground, electric power network systems.
Many Passamaquoddies could be plugged
Into the invisible underground,
Transcontinental, time-zone spanning,
Electric energy network integration
And thence relayed to Alaska
While picking up Canadian Rockies water power
Along the way.
The integrated North American network
Could not only be trans-linked
Through Mexico and Central America
Into an Amazon-to-be-powered
South American network
But also across the Bering Straits
From Alaska to Russia
To join with their now completed
Eastern extension of Western Russia's network
Powered by northward flowing, into-the-Arctic
Siberian river systems.
This now feasible, intercontinental network
Would integrate America, Asia and Europe
And integrate the night-and-day, spherically cycling
Shadow-and-light zones of Planet Earth
And this would occasion the 24-hour use
Of the now only fifty per cent of the time used
World-around standby generator capacity
Whose fifty per cent unused capacities
Heretofore were mandatorily required
Only for peakload servicing of local non-interconnected
    energy users.
Such intercontinental network integration
Would overnight double the already-installed and in-use,
Electric power generating capacity of our Planet.

And lying well within
The progressive 1,500 mile hookup reachability
From an American-Russian power integration
Are the intercontinental networks of China,
    India and Africa.


It is everywhere around the world
Incontrovertibly documented
That as the local kilowatt hours
Of distributed electrical energy increase
The local birth rate
Is commensurably diminished and longevity increases.
In respect to any of its specific geographical areas,
The birth rate of that area
Trends in inverse proportion
To electrical energy generation and distribution
The sudden world population bulge
Which has occasioned
Dire population increase predictions
Was occasioned first by the failure to die
Of those who used to die
And secondly by the continued new birth acceleration
Only within the world's
As yet non-industrialized countries.
As world industrialization will be completed
By twentieth-century's end
The ever-diminishing birth rate
Of the industrial countries
Will bring about world population stabilization
By 2000 A.D.


Universe has no pollution.
All the chemistries of the Universe are essential

168

To its comprehensive self-regeneration.
The ninety-two regenerative chemical elements
Associate, disassociate and intertransform
In a wide range of time-lag rates.
All the dumped chemistries
Spoken of ignorantly as "pollution" or "waste"
Are always needed *elsewhere*
In the intelligent integration
Of world-around energy regenerating economics.
All the sulphur emitted annually
From the world's industrial chimneys
Exactly equal to the amount of sulphur
Being taken annually to keep industry going.

And while the byproduct chemistries
Are in high concentration
Before going out the stacks or nozzles
They can be economically distributed
To their elsewhere-needed functioning.
After leaving the stacks or nozzles
The byproduct chemicals are so diffuse
As to be economically unrecoverable.
In their diffuse state the byproducts
Often become toxic
To various biological species,
The ultimate overall costs of which to humanity
May easily be the cessation of terrestrial life.

Yesterday's preoccupation with major energy harnessing
Primarily for the killing of humans by humans
Now can be comprehensively redirected
To intelligent and responsible production
Of a total-humanity sustaining system.

169

Swift realization of all the foregoingly considered
Epochal transition of human affairs
From a "might" to a "right"
Accounted and inspired
World economics
Is now scheduled for swift realization
By inexorable evolutionary events
To be accompanied by maximum social stresses
With only one alternative outcome
To its total human advantaging—
The alternative is human extinction
Aboard our Planet.

All thinking humanity young or old
Not only will condone
Reversal of public position taking
When it is predicated upon
Better and more inclusive information
Than was at first available
In fact it will think even more favorably
Of the integrity
Of those who admit error for humanity's sake
At the risk of losing previous political support.
So well informed is the young society
Which now is taking the world initiative
That only such integrity of long distance thinking
And unselfish preoccupation
Can win its support.

I pray you will make your stand
Swiftly and unambiguously clear
As being against any further incursions
Of petroleum into Maine

Or of pipelines in Alaska.
I pray that you will concurrently
Initiate resumption of Passamaquoddy
Together with initiation of a plurality
Of such Fundy tidal energy convertors
With combined capacities
Sufficient for celestial-energy support
Of all human life aboard our Planet
To be maintained successfully
Until Earth-based humanity
Has successfully migrated
Into larger cosmic neighborhood functioning.

# TEN PROPOSALS FOR IMPROVING THE WORLD

## TEN PROPOSALS FOR
## IMPROVING THE WORLD

The intellect, vision and courage of Mahatma Gandhi conceived of passive resistance with which bloodless revolution he broke the hold on India of history's most powerful sovereignty. Passive resistance will not amplify the production of life support.

In extension of the Mahatma's magnificent vision we are committed to the design science revolution by which it is possible bloodlessly to raise the standard of living of all humanity to a higher level of physical and metaphysical satisfaction than that hitherto experienced or dreamed of by any humans. All the knowledge and resources are now available with which to accomplish that comprehensive success.

This can all be realized by 1985 without any individual profiting at the expense of others or interfering with another's enjoyment of total planetary citizenship. It requires the competent design science commitment of world-around youth to realize the Gandhian integrity.

Youth's spontaneously mutual commitment can only be inspired through experientially gained knowledge and love-sustained innate faith in the eternal reliability of cosmically manifest principles as discovered by science.

175

The world-around problems that have to be solved by bloodless design science revolution are:

## Education Revolution: The Highest Priority of All

An education revolution based on synergy, which means
behavior of whole systems unpredicted by behavior of any of
its parts taken separately, requires the reversal of our present
system of compartmentation of knowledge and of going from
the particular toward the ever more special.

We must commence education with the inventory of all
known, i.e., all as-yet-discovered, generalized principles and
proceed from that whole to the realization of special cases.
This calls for the elimination of all specialization, with gener-
alists in limited-period plunges-in-depth to special case studies
and applications of the omni-interaccommodative generalized
principles. Plunges in depth involve unique subcomplexes of
the whole. These generate the applied sciences.

The education revolution requires the elimination of exclusively academic tenure. All of humanity must be given
lifelong research fellowship tenure. All objective work must be
spontaneously inspired and co-operatively initiated as with
children's games. Participation on all "varsity" production and
service playing teams must be attained through demonstrated
competence.

Learning is to be accomplished by use of cassette-tape type
video documentation with the individual child learning to find
the most competent answers to the child's own questions. It is
programed by the child who spontaneously presses the obvious symbol buttons: Why is the sky blue?

## Conversion of World Accounting System

The world accounting system must be converted from annual agricultural metabolics to an eternal world-around accounting which includes all generations to come, and which is consistent with the cosmic economics of an eternally regenerative physical universal system. The accounting system would include a redefinition of wealth with the scarcity model of economics to be made obsolete by the magnitude of man's participation in the irreversible amplification of the inventory of information: i.e., know-how. This eliminates economic competition.

As a by-product of the new accounting system, competition for the monopoly of affection may also be surrendered along with the onerousness of ownership.

We must advance from an inherently depreciative to an inherently appreciative commonwealth.

The Universe is not operating on a basis in which the Star Sun opines ignorantly that it can no longer afford to let Earth have the energy to keep life going because it hasn't paid its last bill: "We Stars have got to make a profit!" The cosmic accounting assumes omnivalidity. Humanity must eliminate the requirement of "Earning the right to live." Living for all at high standard must be accredited. Work and right-to-live must be divorced. Work must be considered the greatest human privilege.

## Elimination of Property by Making Ownership Onerous

The elimination of property by making ownership onerous is to be accomplished by making man a world citizen, each to enjoy all the treasures of the whole Earth. He can't any more "take it with him" around the world than he could "take it with him" in yesterday's concept of "into the next world." He "can't take it with him" and enjoy the new world of Universe citizenship, and its natural emancipation from slavery chained to ponderous thingness.

## World Democracy by Electronic Referendum

World democracy is to be incorruptibly accommodated by continual electronic referendum, being progressively fed by subconsciously telepathic ultra-ultra- high frequency electromagnetic wave propagation, signalling subconsciously reflexed feedback attitudes toward specific propositions coping with evolutionary problems as educationally manifest.

## Elimination of All World Sovereignties

All the customs barriers disappear as man goes from guarding the local roots of his originally exclusive agrarian metabolics life support into a world-around imperishable metals-sustaining impoundment of cosmic energy, and eternally regenerative energy, labeled industrialization in the world economy.

The high performance necessary to sustaining all life can only be realized by free access to all sources everywhere.

## Theoretical Exploration Through World Game

World War gaming considers total use of total resources only for the maintenance of killingry in support of unilateral survival, on the mistaken a priori assumption of fundamental inadequacy of planetary life support. World gaming discovers the inventory of metaphysical capabilities can amplify the life support effectiveness of the inventors of physical resources to accommodate all humanity.

The 92 regenerative chemical elements themselves are non-dissipatable and are only re-circulatable. The energy of Universe is eternally regenerative and inexhaustible. The metaphysical resource always increases. The game is "How to make humanity a successful member of successful Universe?"

## Realization of Design Science Competence

How to continually employ the total context of known generalized principles and resource inventory in realizing ever higher magnitudes of performance satisfaction loaded into each recirculation of the imperishable chemical element associations and reassociations. How to do so much with so little in support of total ecology as to render all humanity economically and physiologically successful.

## Recognition of Humanity's Unique Functioning in Universe

Humanity's unique antientropic functioning in Universe is as a metaphysically advantaged problem solver. Universe needs man's intellectual capability which discovers some of the eternal laws operating in total Universe and applies them to local problem solving. That is our only meaning to each other.

### Identification of Mathematical Coordinate System of Universe

An apparently comprehensive mathematical coordinate system of Universe provides modelable conceptualization of science which is experimentally demonstrable. This realization of conceptualization will reunite the sciences and the humanities.

### Philosophical Realization that Physical Is Not Life

The philosophical realization that the physical is not life will lead to the ultimate conquest of mind over muscle. This generates the historical transition of experience to a predominant mind-over-matter reality.

Misassuming that both the animate and inanimate are physical, humanity misidentified "civilization" with the burial of its dead. That is where man broke away from all the animals. Animals recognize that the carcass is not life. Kings sought to rationalize the inheritability of sovereignty by identifying life with the physical. This also generated middle class mausoleums and hereditary privileges.

Emancipation of individuality requires elimination of the slave mentality. It is the realization of the inherently inviolable integrity of the individual.